Gardens to Visit in Britain

Publishers' Note
The times of opening of the gardens described in this book are liable to be changed annually, and although these are correct at the time of going to press we would recommend that any intending visitor checks beforehand (see reference to relevant annual publications in the Foreword).

Gardens
to Visit in
Britain
Arthur Hellyer

PAUL HAMLYN
LONDON NEW YORK SYDNEY TORONTO

Published by
The Hamlyn Publishing Group Limited

LONDON · NEW YORK · SYDNEY · TORONTO

Hamlyn House Feltham Middlesex England

© Arthur Hellyer 1970

Printed by

Lee Fung Printing Company Limited

Hong Kong

ISBN 0 600 44179 2

Contents

Foreword

Though gardening for pleasure and display started comparatively late in the British Isles, it has developed so successfully and in so many different ways that today British gardens are famous throughout the world. The best gardens, opened frequently to the public, have become an important tourist attraction and, at home, garden visiting has become an accepted part of our way of life. It has been enormously encouraged by the enterprise of certain charitable institutions and the ready co-operation of garden owners, who for a small charge open their gardens to the public and give the proceeds to charity.

However, most of these gardens only open very occasionally. The labour and expense involved in getting them into peak condition and the disruption of the normal usage of the garden are too great to be faced frequently, and the openings are usually restricted to one, or at most two, afternoons per year. Nor, since the arrangements are reviewed annually with the charities concerned, can one be certain more than a few months ahead what those dates of opening may be or whether they will be fixed at all, since new gardens are added and old ones fall out each year.

For these reasons I have not thought it wise to include any of these casually opened gardens in this book, which is intended primarily for tourists and others with a fairly serious interest in garden visiting. It can cause considerable inconvenience and even annoyance to private owners to have visitors turning up on days when their gardens are not open, and since the correct dates and times are freely available in the annually renewed guides of the charities involved, this is where information about them is best obtained. In particular, the guide of The National Gardens Scheme, the 'yellow book', should be obtained; and also that of the Gardeners' Sunday Organisation, the 'green book'. Both will be found on most newspaper and book-stalls from early spring onwards or can be obtained direct from the charities concerned, The National Gardens Scheme, 57 Lower Belgrave Street, London, S.W.1, and The Gardeners' Sunday Organisation, White Witches, Claygate Road, Dorking, Surrey. Another extremely useful book which lists both dates and times of opening is *Properties of the National Trust*. This can be obtained from The National Trust, 42 Queen Anne's Gate, London, S.W.1.

In this book I am concerned with the gardens that, whether privately or publicly owned, are open fairly frequently and regularly. They are the gardens on which anyone planning anything like an extended tour of British gardens should base an itinerary, and I have attempted to give sufficient information about each and to support that information by sufficient illustrations both to enable intending visitors to decide whether this is or is not the kind of garden they would like to see and to provide a useful record and reminder of the gardens visited in after years.

But, in addition to these easily visited gardens, there are a great many casually opened gardens that are extremely beautiful or interesting and few that will not give considerable pleasure to the garden lover, since the charity organisers are careful to exclude inferior gardens. I therefore strongly recommend all garden visitors to obtain the various lists and guides to these gardens and to make a point of seeing such as may be open at times and in places convenient to their itineraries.

ARTHUR HELLYER

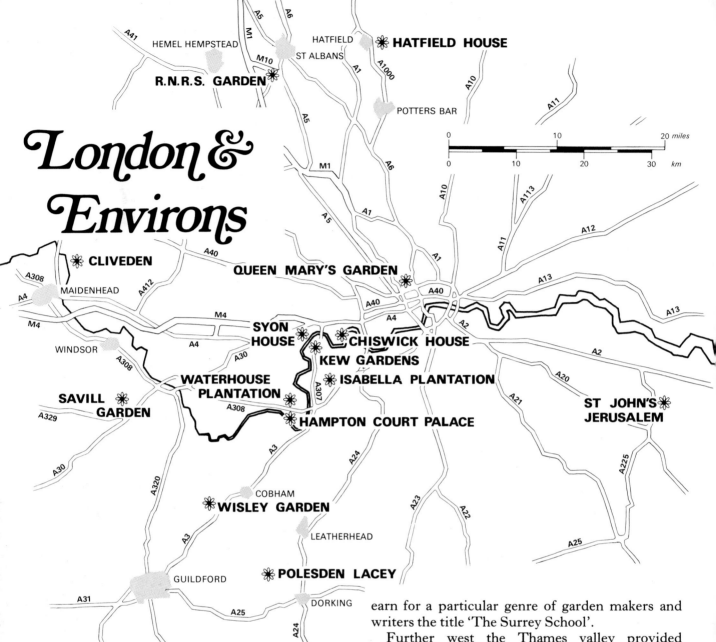

London & Environs

HEMEL HEMPSTEAD

A41

A5 A6

M1

M10

HATFIELD
ST ALBANS

A1

✻ HATFIELD HOUSE

A1000

A10

A11

POTTERS BAR

R.N.R.S. GARDEN ✻

A5

M1

A6

A10

A11

A11

A12

A1

A40

✻ CLIVEDEN

A308

MAIDENHEAD

A412

QUEEN MARY'S GARDEN ✻

A40

A1

A113

A13

A13

A13

A4

M4

A40

M4

M4

A4

A40

WINDSOR

A308

A4

SYON ✻
HOUSE

A30

✻ CHISWICK HOUSE

KEW GARDENS ✻

A2

A2

A2

WATERHOUSE
PLANTATION ✻

A307

✻ ISABELLA PLANTATION

A20

SAVILL ✻
GARDEN

A329

A308

A308

✻ HAMPTON COURT PALACE

A21

ST JOHN'S ✻
JERUSALEM

A225

A3

A320

A24

A23

A22

A25

A30

✻ WISLEY GARDEN

COBHAM

A3

LEATHERHEAD

A25

GUILDFORD

A31

✻ POLESDEN LACEY

A25

DORKING

A24

A3

✻ WINKWORTH ARBORETUM

*I*t is fortunate for those who have to earn their living in London that to the south and west is some of the best gardening country in Britain. Much of the soil of Surrey and some of adjacent Berkshire is sandy and agriculturally rather poor, but it is also lime free and highly suitable for the cultivation of a great many trees and shrubs including the highly decorative rhododendrons and azaleas. Birch woods abound, heather covers much of the common land and there are sufficient streams to make it easy to include water in the garden scheme.

It is in these surroundings that the great gardens such as Wisley and the Windsor Great Park trio, the Savill Garden, Valley Garden and Punch Bowl, have grown up almost as though native to the site. Here, too, Gertrude Jekyll carried out her experiments in permanent plant associations which were to revolutionise 20th-century gardening and

earn for a particular genre of garden makers and writers the title 'The Surrey School'.

Further west the Thames valley provided equally congenial though quite different gardening conditions. Here the tradition is older, going back to the 16th century with Hampton Court, followed by Syon House, the great botanic gardens of Kew, Cliveden and many other stately houses standing in suitably impressive gardens or parks.

Moving northwards and eastwards one quickly reaches the chalk and limestone of the Chiltern Hills where beech woods abound and the countryside is of great natural beauty, though the soil is less adaptable for the cultivation of ornamental plants because of its generally rather high lime content.

But in Hertfordshire to the north we are back in excellent gardening soil and good gardens abound. Here, near St Albans, the Royal National Rose Society has made its fine rose display and trial garden, and not far away at Hatfield House is what remains of one of the great Jacobean gardens with more recent additions which increase the richness and variety of its planting.

Kurume azaleas in the Isabella Plantation

Chiswick House

**Chiswick, London. In Burlington Lane, Chiswick.
Ministry of Public Building and Works. The
grounds are open daily throughout the year.**

The garden of Chiswick House is important historically
as a link in the chain of development between the formal French style of the 17th century and the informal
landscape gardening which was popular in Britain in
the mid-18th century.

Chiswick House itself was designed by the Earl of
Burlington, a leader of artistic taste in the early 18th
century, as a place in which to display his pictures and
other art treasures, and he engaged Charles Bridgeman
and William Kent to assist in planning the garden.
The result was a somewhat odd mixture of stiff
avenues radiating in the, then popular, goosefoot
pattern, wiggly paths through woodland and shrub-
bery, statues of Roman emperors displayed against
an exedra or semi-circle formed of clipped yew, and a
water course first designed as an ornamental canal and
later changed to a more natural, river-like course.

Much of the original Chiswick House garden has been
built over, but sufficient remains to give a very good
idea of what it originally was. All had fallen into dis-
repair until taken over by the London Borough of
Hounslow which now cares for the garden and has
nearly completed an accurate restoration of it to the
original designs. The buildings and temples, too, some
designed by Kent, are being restored by the Ministry of
Public Building and Works, and more recent additions
to the garden, such as the large conservatory and
Victorian parterre have been well planted and are gay
with flowers throughout the season.

Cliveden

**Taplow, Berkshire. Three miles north of Maiden-
head, on the B476 from Taplow to Wooburn. The
National Trust. Open from Wednesday to Sunday
and on Bank Holiday Mondays from early April
to the end of October.**

This famous mansion, designed by Sir Charles Barry in
the mid-19th century, stands on a great plateau of land
levelled a hundred years earlier for another house
which was destroyed by fire. It is high above the
Thames, ringed by woods except to the south, where it
is open to the river, and to the north, from which side
the house is approached by a very wide straight drive
flanked by mown grass. From either side the view is
impressive. A stone-balustraded terrace on the south
side of the house is so high above the immensely long
parterre below, with the river in the middle distance,
that one has somewhat the feeling of standing on the
bridge of a great ship looking down on the deck and the
sea beyond. The beds of the parterre are large and
simple, in keeping with its character, and the whole
is cut across at the house end by a handsome stone and
brick balustrade, brought from the Villa Borghese in
Rome late in the 19th century.

At the head of the approach drive to the north stands an
immense marble shell surrounded by figures, the whole
contained in a circular stone water basin. A straight
avenue cut through the wood to the west permits a view

of a large stone vase on a pedestal, an invitation to explore a whole series of smaller avenues which crisscross the woodland, revealing new vistas, ornaments and buildings. The drive itself leads into a large rectangular forecourt enclosed by walls on three sides and the house on the fourth. Here there are some simple rectangles of grass flanked by flower borders and with a number of elaborate stone sarcophagi.

From the parterre a path leads around the western lip of the hilltop, at times skirting the woods, at times plunging into them, with views of the river, one of the finest of which is from Canning's oak. This walk passes a little open-air theatre, where it is said Rule Britannia was first played, to a classical temple, the Blenheim Pavilion, and finally to a Long Garden which leads back to the entrance drive. This Long Garden is itself a kind of decorated avenue, patterned in box edging with topiary specimens and delightful small statues.

At a little distance, entirely separate from these other points of interest, is a large water garden with Japanese features, principal among which is a gay little pagoda acquired from the Great Exhibition of 1851, and now standing on an island. There is great variety in the planting of trees, shrubs and herbaceous plants around this garden.

Hatfield House

Hatfield, Hertfordshire. South of Hatfield close to the A1000. Privately owned. West Gardens open every weekday from Easter Saturday until the first Sunday in October and on Sundays from May to early October. The East and West Gardens are open on Mondays from May to the end of September.

Above. The permanently planted parterre at Hatfield House with the Bishop's Palace in the background

Opposite. The main avenue at Chiswick House, an early example of the work of William Kent. What remains of the original garden is being restored

Below. The view from the south terrace at Cliveden over the parterre with the Thames beyond

Hatfield House, built early in the 17th century, is one of the great houses of England and it is for its architectural splendours, the richness of its furnishings and the interest of the Great Hall of the former Palace of the Bishops of Ely, which now stands near it on lower ground, that it is mainly visited. Yet the gardens which surround and link the two buildings are also of great interest and beauty. Over the centuries they have seen many changes, but have retained much of the formal character which, no doubt, they originally had. There are three separate parterres, the one to the west being the most elaborate both in design and planting. It is enclosed by a yew hedge, has a central circular pool and fountain, and its rather crowded beds are planted with

a medley of shrubs, roses, herbaceous plants and annuals, rather in the manner of a cottage garden. It is viewed to best advantage from the raised terrace which separates it from the house.

The smaller parterre in front of the Old Palace is more open in design and is largely planted with roses. To the east of Hatfield House is a third parterre leading to a fine maze, said to have been made in the 19th century. Even this does not complete the tale of the Hatfield gardens since there are also fine herbaceous borders backed by a high brick wall, various flower beds and borders and an extensive woodland garden to the south-west of the house. The last is at its best in spring when rhododendrons and azaleas are in bloom.

Hampton Court

Hampton, Middlesex. Beside the River Thames on the A308 from Kingston to Staines. Ministry of Public Building and Works. Open daily throughout the year except for Christmas Day, Boxing Day and Good Friday.

This magnificent palace, started by Cardinal Wolsey in 1514, has been greatly altered and added to during the ensuing centuries and its gardens have also seen numerous changes. Wolsey created a garden in the style of his day with a 'mount', complete with galleries and arbours, a labyrinth and beds of flowers enclosed by wooden posts and rails painted in different colours. Nothing now remains of this garden which was obliterated by Charles II to make way for a design by André Mollet. This incorporated the famous goosefoot of the three avenues radiating from a semi-circle centred on the east front of the building, and forms the basis of the plan to the present day. But, whereas in Stuart times the semi-circle itself was filled by an elaborate parterre, to-day it is an area largely turfed, the lines of the avenues strongly accentuated by yew trees clipped into broad-based cones. There are beds filled with dahlias, pelargoniums, heliotropes, fuchsias, and other flowers in season, but these play a subsidiary role, interest being concentrated on the tree-lined avenues themselves which, beyond the formal circle, extend through the park almost to the outskirts of Kingston.

The central avenue is filled with an immense canal, the Long Water, stretching away into the far distance and providing a suitably noble vista from the palace and also delightful viewpoints and reflections of it when seen in the opposite direction. A Broad Walk flanked by herbaceous borders completes this part of the design, making the base of the semi-circle and continuing on either side to the Thames on the south, and to the Flower Pot Gate on the Kingston Road to the north.

Later hands have added other features. Great favourites with visitors are the small formal gardens to the south, collectively known as the Tudor Gardens, though two were actually planned in the 18th century, while the third is a 20th-century addition in the style of a Tudor knot garden. These are heavily planted, one in the Dutch style with much topiary and bedding plants in season, another as a Renaissance garden, and all are gay with flowers throughout the spring and summer.

However, the old Privy Garden which separates the Tudor Gardens from the Broad Walk remains in outline as in Mollet's plan, but its elaborate parterres have been replaced by large beds of flowering shrubs, intersected by grass paths and terminated by an elaborate wrought-iron screen designed by Jean Tijou. The vinery is famous for the size and age of its single vine; the maze is a modern version of Wolsey's labyrinth, and to the north of the palace is the so-called Wilderness which is really a good example of modern tree and shrub planting to an open plan. From the Lion Gate, in this part of the garden, a view can be obtained of the great double avenue of chestnuts in Bushy Park on the other side of the Kingston Road.

Finally, where Tudor knights once jousted in a tilt-yard, a large rose garden has been made, well stocked and maintained with a number of modern varieties which add their usual long season of colour and interest to the gardens.

The Pond Garden at Hampton Court, made in the Dutch style

Winkworth Arboretum

Godalming, Surrey. Three miles south-east of Godalming on the B2130 to Cranleigh. The National Trust. Open daily throughout the year.

This fine tree collection covers 95 acres and is well sited on a curving hillside with a stream and lake in the valley below. The collection was privately made by Dr Wilfred Fox and given by him to the National Trust in 1952. The arrangement is entirely informal with no very obvious attempt to secure landscape effects, though some shrubs, notably azaleas, hydrangeas and cotoneasters, have been grouped to give a mass display at their respective seasons. But the natural beauty of the site is so great, and the trees and shrubs so well chosen, that this arboretum is always admired even by those visitors who have little knowledge of arboriculture. It is at its loveliest in spring when the bluebells form a carpet beneath the trees, and in autumn when the colouring of the leaves can be very brilliant.

Above. Autumn at Winkworth Arboretum. Maples of many kinds, sweet gums and sumachs give some of the finest leaf colours at this season

Below. The Long Water reflecting the East Front, Hampton Court

Isabella Plantation

Richmond Park, Richmond, Surrey. Situated within the triangle formed by the Robin Hood Gate, Kingston Gate and Ham Gate and most readily reached by car from the large car park half-a-mile south-west of Robin Hood Gate. Crown Property. Open daily throughout the year.

This beautiful garden has been made in a roughly oval area of woodland which lies in a shallow saucer of land. Two small streams run through it, converging midway and finally flowing into a lake outside the wood, and two smaller lakes have been made within the woodland. Around the streams the woodland has been sufficiently thinned to permit underplanting with rhododendrons, azaleas, magnolias, camellias, hydrangeas and other shrubs that enjoy semi-shade, and the stream sides have been planted with primulas, astilbes, irises, hostas, ferns and many other plants. Because of the character of the planting, the garden is at its most brilliant in May and early June when it is a great attraction to flower lovers, but the plants are so well disposed, and the situation so remote and peaceful, that it can be visited with pleasure at any time of the year.

Polesden Lacey

near Great Bookham, Surrey. One-and-a-half miles south of Great Bookham on the road to Box Hill. The National Trust. Open on Wednesdays, Saturdays, Sundays and Bank Holiday Mondays from March to mid-December, also on Tuesdays (not following a Bank Holiday) from May to August.

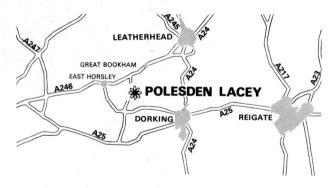

Garden making at Polesden Lacey has been carried out at two periods, separated by 150 years, but neither coincides with the date of the building of the present Regency villa, between 1821 and 1824. It had been preceded by a simple Caroline house, and the first landscape garden had been started for this about 1761. The site, a broad and shallow valley running roughly from west to east with the house placed well up on the north slope, was admirably suited for the purpose and

One of the two flower-lined streams which flow through the Isabella Plantation in Richmond Park. It is at its most colourful in May and June

can have needed little 'improvement'. No doubt more trees were added but the most obvious and impressive addition of this period is a raised walk which follows the middle contour of the valley for a considerable distance, permitting uninterrupted yet changing views of the scenery. It is essentially a formal feature, reminiscent of the grass terrace at Muncaster Castle (see p. 124) and serving a similar purpose. Like the Muncaster terrace, it has a low trimmed hedge on its 'viewing' side and is backed by woodland, but it is diversified by bays, with large stone urns, and has two stone pillars at its west end and a Doric portico at its east end, all of which emphasise its formal intention. This walk was extended in the early 19th century by Richard Brinsley Sheridan when he was living at Polesden Lacey.

To the south of the house a wide lawn sweeps down to a low hedge trimmed like a battlement, and there are fine cedars, blue spruces and other trees to the sides, where they do not interfere with the view. To the west a whole series of new gardens has been made in the present century; mostly intimate, enclosed and ornamented gardens rather in the manner of outdoor rooms, though some are more open in character, and one steep bank has been left more or less in its natural state clothed with spreading junipers, barberries and other shrubs. One of the small gardens is planted mainly with lavender, another with roses and a third with irises, and one area near the house is completely enclosed in clipped yew against which statues are displayed. This was planned as her own burial place by Dame Margaret Helen Greville who lived at Polesden Lacey from 1906 until her death in 1944.

Above. Another view in the Isabella Plantation. Evergreen azaleas are planted in fine drifts of a kind to create a magnificent contrast in colours

Below. The walk through the formal gardens at Polesden Lacey, each enclosed by a hedge of box or yew, giving each the character of an outdoor room

Kew Gardens

Kew, Surrey. Just south of Kew Bridge off the M4 at the junction with the North and South Circular Roads. Ministry of Public Building and Works. Open daily throughout the year, except Christmas Day.

So many famous names have been linked with the planning of Kew Gardens, so various have been their aims and so mixed the origins of the gardens themselves, that it would not have been surprising had they emerged as a hotch-potch of styles. That instead they are one of the most beautiful of British gardens, as well as one of the greatest botanical gardens in the world, is due to the skill with which both the various parts have been welded together and the scientific work of the garden has been kept within an overall design that is entirely satisfying to the eye.

There were originally two gardens at Kew belonging to different houses and owners. To the west, beside the River Thames, was the garden of Richmond Lodge which was largely laid out by Queen Caroline, wife of George II, while to the east was the garden of Kew House, which was very largely made by George II's son Frederick, Prince of Wales, and his even more garden-minded wife, Augusta. It was not until their son, George III, inherited both properties after his mother's death in 1771 that they were merged, and the lane that separated them was closed in 1783.

But before this date William Kent and Sir William Chambers had both been engaged in the design of the Kew House gardens; Chambers being responsible for a number of the classical and romantic buildings which still adorn it, including the towering Pagoda which makes so prominent a focal point at the south end, the handsome Orangery at the north end, and the Temple of Aeolus built in the form of a little rotunda on a hillock which occupies another key position near the eastern boundary.

Meanwhile, at Richmond Lodge, George III had been employing the great exponent of landscape gardening, Lancelot Brown, to redesign much of the garden. Brown made the artificial valley running parallel with the river, which has now become the rhododendron dell; but though the long lake which nearly bisects this part of the garden and provides some of Kew's loveliest views has been attributed to Brown, it seems unlikely that he planned it.

Yet a fourth famous garden designer was concerned with Kew during the mid-19th century, W. A. Nesfield, a prime mover in the Italian revival of that period. He it was who began to give the various parts unity by his skilful placing of main walks and vistas and his siting of the huge Palm House and the slightly smaller Temperate House both designed by Decimus Burton. But unity was also conferred in another way: the disposition of the thousands of trees and shrubs required for Kew's botanical collection. A private botanical collection had already been started by the Princess Augusta, who engaged William Aiton for this purpose in 1759. George III appointed Sir Joseph Banks to superintend the combined gardens, and this speeded the collection of exotic plants; but it was not until the gardens became national property in 1840 and Sir Joseph Hooker was appointed their first Director, that the flow became a flood. Before this, the botanical collection had been confined to a small area near the north-east corner of the gardens where the species beds and the greenhouses for specialist collections are still found. Hooker and his successors needed far more room and eventually had to spread their fine trees and shrubs throughout the whole 300 acres of the combined gardens. In doing so they observed a definite progression in density of planting, placing the trees mainly as isolated specimens towards the north and east, where the design was already more formal, but gradually thickening to a woodland density in the south and west, where wide grass walks take the place of gravelled paths. It is a progression so gradual and natural that the casual visitor is almost unaware of it, yet it serves as the perfect flux for the disparate ingredients of this great garden.

*Above. Crocuses by Kew Palace, and (below)
the famous Palm House at Kew, built in 1844
Opposite top. The figure fountain in Queen Mary's
Garden, and bottom, some of the rose beds by the lake*

Queen Mary's Garden

Regent's Park, London. In the Inner Circle of Regent's Park. Ministry of Public Building and Works. Open daily throughout the year.

When John Nash designed Regent's Park in the early years of the 19th century with the intention of building in it a palace for the Prince Regent, he planned two avenues at right angles to one another, the shorter terminating in a perfect circle contained within one curve of a large lake. This became the Inner Circle, and for many years it contained a botanic garden. But, early in the 1930s, it was decided to establish in it a rose garden, partly as a new amenity for the park and partly to help the British rose growing industry. It has served both ends so well that it is now one of the most famous and beautiful rose gardens in the world, in which many of the newest varieties can be seen flourishing.

The garden started as little more than a circle of rose beds enclosed by pillars and ropes on which climbing roses were trained. It then occupied only a small part of the Inner Circle, but it has proved so popular a feature that it has frequently been extended and is now four or five times its original size with 40,000 rose bushes growing in it.

The Inner Circle contains a small lake of its own and the original rose garden was placed near it. The main extension has been along the line of this lake and then on, following the curve of the Inner Circle, to cross the main avenue and terminate at a restaurant built in the style of a pavilion.

However, even this has not proved sufficient. Large rose beds now flank the avenue itself where it leads to a water basin containing a large bronze statue of Venus attended by cupids and a youth. Sturdy roses and rose species that can be grown as shrubs are also gradually being planted right round the perimeter of the Inner Circle, and there are interesting experiments in underplanting them with small shrubs and perennials to lengthen the season of interest.

Almost all the roses in Queen Mary's Garden are planted in large beds, each devoted to one variety. These are frequently renewed and replanted so that the collection is always up to date. The setting with the lake, its attendant rock garden and a background of trees, is delightful and very different from the formal surroundings of most rose gardens. Above all, the roses in Queen Mary's Garden are supremely well grown and, when at their flowering peaks in June, July and September, are a sight to remember.

Syon House

Brentford, Middlesex. Between Brentford and Isleworth, entrance from London Road and Park Road (off Twickenham Road). The Gardening Centre Ltd. Open daily from March to October and on Saturdays and Sundays only from November to February.

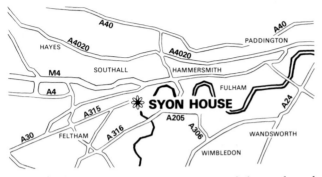

The Gardening Centre occupies part of the park and garden of Syon House, one of the famous stately homes of England, and its intention is to bring together in one place all that is best in British horticulture in plants and equipment. For this purpose it contains exhibition buildings and commercial displays, but in this book we are concerned with the garden only. This falls into three sections. The central one comprises a big parterre partially enfolded in the curving wings of a large, beautiful conservatory built by Charles Fowler in the 1820s. The dome is of ironwork and is said to be the first use of glass and iron for this purpose, a precursor of the great glass and iron structures made by Sir Joseph Paxton in the following decades.

To the east is a river-like lake constructed by Lancelot Brown and fed from the River Thames, which at this point separates Syon from Kew. Brown's 18th-century landscaping has been enriched by generations of tree planting and the garden contains magnificent specimens of many exotic trees including especially fine swamp cypresses (taxodium). Towards the end of this section is a statue of the goddess Flora on a tall column. This fine landscape and tree garden is the setting for the main display buildings of The Gardening Centre, and many island beds have been introduced to permit a much more varied planting with trees, shrubs, herbaceous perennials and some annuals and bedding plants.

To the west of Syon House an entirely new 6-acre rose garden has been made to display the best new varieties. This is partly paved and partly set in grass, with a curving stone-pillared pergola for climbers. From this rose garden the finest views are obtained of Syon House and of the water meadows beside the Thames.

Above. The lake at Syon House, designed in the 18th century by Lancelot (Capability) Brown. Many fine trees, shrubs and hardy plants have been added since

Opposite top. The beautiful conservatory by Charles Fowler at Syon House was built in the early 19th century and is one of the first buildings of its kind

Opposite bottom. A splendid Cedar of Lebanon beside the moat which surrounds the garden at St John's Jerusalem

St John's Jerusalem

Sutton-at-Hone, Kent. Three miles south of Dartford on the A225 to Farningham. The National Trust. Open every Wednesday.

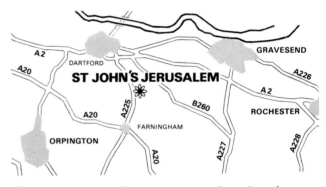

This property is of interest to antiquarians because it contains a room that, in the 13th century, was a chapel of the Commandery of the Knights Hospitallers. It is said that Henry III often stayed there, and across the meadow which separates it from the road, can be seen a broad depression marking the position of the original entrance road by which he must have approached.

To gardeners its interest lies mainly in the fact that its large, more or less rectangular garden is entirely surrounded by water drawn from the River Darent, which flows beside it. This has given opportunity for planting a fine collection of willows, including many with coloured bark, which are pollarded annually to obtain the best effect. One weeping willow was grown from a cutting taken from the tree under which Napoleon was buried on St Helena, and there are other trees with similar historic interest.

A very large cedar stands by the entrance to the forecourt garden which is enclosed by hedges. From this, long twin borders lead through the vegetable garden to a cross walk following the bank of the river. This walk is bordered with daffodils which are also naturalised in great quantities in a little orchard. Peonies grow well in this garden, and so does the Crown Imperial, *Fritillaria imperialis*.

Wisley Garden

Ripley, Surrey. Two-and-a-half miles north-east of Ripley off the A3 from London to Guildford. The Royal Horticultural Society. Open daily throughout the year, except Christmas Day and Good Friday. Sundays are reserved for Fellows of the R.H.S.

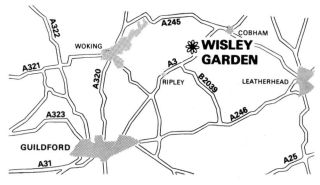

This is one of the very great gardens of Britain, and one of the largest in extent, covering about 150 acres, excluding the 6 acres devoted to vegetable trials. The house, now used as laboratories, class-rooms and offices, was originally a pleasant country residence built in the 19th-century neo-Tudor style and surrounded by gardens laid out by George F. Wilson who acquired the property in the 1870s. The main feature then was the wild garden made in natural oak woodland to the west of the house, and this part remains a particularly delightful feature in spring when the rhododendrons, azaleas, daffodils, anemones and many other plants are in bloom.

In 1903, after Mr Wilson's death, the property was given to the Royal Horticultural Society and has since been extended both north and south, partly as a permanent garden to demonstrate the ornamental use of various plants, partly as a trial ground for new flower and vegetable varieties. It has not always been easy to combine the two requirements without interfering with the overall effect of the garden, and one of the more recent changes has been the removal of the greenhouses, which originally stood in front of the house, to a more distant position so that the landscaping of this important section could be improved.

Among the most admired ornamental features at Wisley are a large rock garden, made on a north-facing slope beside the original wild garden; a large woodland garden on Battleston Hill, an area of rising ground at the south-east corner of the garden; a fine collection of ornamental cherries; long borders, some devoted to herbaceous plants only, others to a mixture of herbaceous plants and shrubs, and some to roses; what is probably the finest example of a heather garden in the British Isles; an extensive pinetum, and two large lakes surrounded by moisture-loving plants. There are also beds reserved for special plants, such as irises, and those that have received the Society's Award of Garden Merit; and, in addition to the greenhouses for tender plants, there are an alpine house and series of alpine frames in which a fine display of rock plants and small bulbous-rooted plants is maintained.

In addition to this, large areas are reserved for the many trials in progress, and those filled with flowers such as delphiniums, dahlias, gladioli, sweet peas and a variety of annuals and other plants add greatly to the gaiety and interest of the garden in spring and summer. There is a good collection of fruit trees, including a model fruit garden, and also two model vegetable gardens and an amateur's greenhouse.

R.N.R.S. Garden

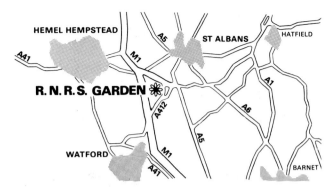

(Bone Hill), Chiswell Green, St Albans, Hertfordshire. Two-and-a-half miles south of St Albans off the A412 to Watford. Royal National Rose Society. Open daily to members only from mid-June to the last Saturday in September, but not on Late Summer Bank Holiday Monday.

This fine garden serves two purposes, one as a display garden for established rose varieties and the other as a trial ground for new varieties. The display garden lies around the house, and the trial ground occupies a field to one side. Here roses are planted in long rectangular beds separated by grass paths, the intention being purely utilitarian though the effect produced when the roses are in full bloom can be exceedingly gay.

By contrast the display garden has been carefully designed to make the maximum visual impact and to illustrate the various ways in which roses can be used. A flagged path is centred on the house, its straight line interrupted by a large circular pool with a central fountain. Wide borders on both sides are filled with floribunda roses planted in large blocks, each of one variety, with green yews, trimmed as narrow columns, well spaced out down the borders, and golden yews trimmed as huge balls behind. On each side of this central feature, numerous large formal beds have been cut out of the lawns and planted with roses, mainly hybrid tea varieties, though a long border which separates the display garden from the trial ground is planted with shrub and old-fashioned roses. The whole of this garden is terminated by a great semi-circular pergola with brick pillars used for the display of climbing roses. There are other smaller sections, probably originally used as vegetable or fruit gardens, but now devoted entirely to roses.

Opposite. The extensive heather garden in the Royal Horticultural Society's garden at Wisley is one of the finest examples of its kind in Britain. These heathers are planted in large drifts of a kind and there is some colour almost throughout the year

Below. Colourful twin borders of floribunda roses in the Royal National Rose Society's display garden and trial grounds, Bone Hill. The contrasted columnar and spherical topiary specimens, which add so much to the design, are of green and golden yew

Above. The peaceful Valley Garden, Windsor Great Park, leads down to Virginia Water and is one of several plantings associated with the Savill Garden

Opposite. A view in the Waterhouse Plantations, Bushy Park. These are very beautiful woodland and glade gardens in which water plays a prominent part

Savill Garden

Savill Garden, Valley Garden and Punch Bowl.

Windsor Great Park, Surrey. One mile west of Englefield Green, off the A30 from Egham to Bagshot. Entrance in Wick Lane. Crown Estate Commissioners. Savill Garden open daily from March to October. The Valley Garden and Punch Bowl are open daily throughout the year.

This garden, together with the Valley Garden and Punch Bowl has been made in the present century under the patronage of the reigning monarch. The Savill Garden is the oldest, work having been started on it in 1932, whereas the Valley Garden and the Punch Bowl were not commenced until after the Second World War.

The Savill Garden, originally mainly a waterside and woodland garden, has grown into an almost complete epitome of what might be called the early 20th-century style, complete with rose garden, herbaceous borders, rock garden and alpine meadow, well-planted walls, streams, pools, woodland and open glades, the whole

now covering about 25 acres. Because of its size, the complexity of its design and the great number of interesting plants it contains, it is highly desirable for the new visitor to obtain a map and guide, and both are available at the gate.

This garden retains its interest throughout the year and has been planned and planted with great skill, the various features, formal and informal, being linked together with considerable ingenuity, and the absence of a house compensated for by the construction of a large wall of old brick as a backing for the formal section. Here, too, will be found a series of raised alpine beds, each filled with soil of a different character so that an exceptional range of plants can be cultivated in them.

The Valley Garden is situated about three-quarters of a mile to the south, past the Obelisk Pond, in a valley leading down to Virginia Water. This is purely a woodland garden, entirely devoid of formal features and most tastefully planted with rhododendrons, azaleas, magnolias, maples, birches and many other choice trees and shrubs. It is one of the most effective landscape gardens planted in recent years.

The Punch Bowl, by contrast, is a supreme *tour de force*, planted mainly to make a stupendous colour impact in late spring. On a semi-circular hillside, a natural amphitheatre, thousands of evergreen azaleas have been massed, intermingled with Japanese maples and other trees which continue to please after the azaleas have finished flowering. It lies to one side of the Valley Garden, and on the other side is the Azalea Valley, mainly planted with modern hybrid deciduous azaleas, in contrast to the evergreen azaleas of the Punch Bowl. Beyond this again is a large and well-conceived heather garden planted with many varieties.

Waterhouse Plantations

Bushy Park, Middlesex. Half-a-mile from the Iron Gates of Hampton Court to the west of the great horse chestnut avenue. Ministry of Public Building and Works. Open every day.

There are two woodland gardens in Bushy Park, but they remain comparatively unknown though they bear comparison with the much more famous woodland gardens in Windsor Great Park and Richmond Park. From the former they differ in having fewer rare plants, and from the latter in occupying a flatter site which has much more water, drawn from the artificial River Longford which flows beside them.

In fact these plantations are almost as much stream and lakeside gardens as they are woodland gardens, and have been designed with considerable skill to make use of the contrasting qualities of quite dense with more open woodland, grassy glades and still or cascading water. There is good contrast in planting, too, some areas being left almost in a natural state, others planted with rhododendrons, azaleas, camellias and other shade-loving shrubs. Like the other two gardens with which they have been compared the Waterhouse Plantations have most colour in May and June but are beautiful in a quieter way at all seasons of the year.

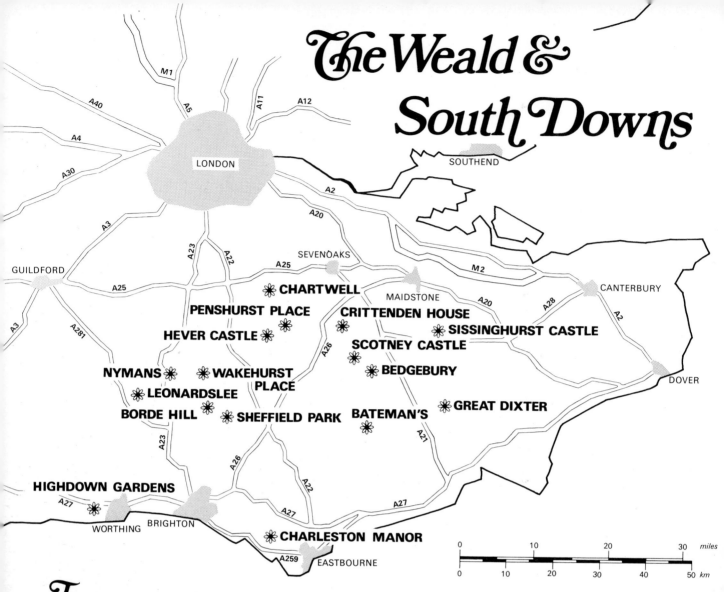

The Weald & South Downs

The Weald extends across a great area of Kent and Sussex, roughly 70 miles in length and 20 miles in breadth, bounded to north and south by chalk hills. It is an area of rich land, full of prosperous farms, and with many orchards and hop gardens in its Kentish section. But it also has another geological peculiarity which has had a considerable influence on the gardens it has produced. Running through it from west to east midway between the North and South Downs and then turning southwards to meet the sea at Hastings, is another smaller hill range with soil of a different character from the chalk of the Downs or the clay of the plain. These are the Forest Ridges, in their south-eastern part becoming the Battle Ridge. Though the soils that occur on them are very varied they include moderately acid sandy loams which are ideal for the cultivation of rhododendrons, azaleas, heathers and similar lime-hating plants.

Moreover, the Ridges are split by steep-sided valleys, some of which provide exceptionally good air drainage, so that on the high land between them many plants can be grown which would be damaged by frost elsewhere in the area. Wakehurst Place, the great collector's garden made by Sir Gerald Loder (later Lord Wakehurst) and now administered by the Royal Botanic Gardens, Kew, occupies just such a situation. Nymans and Leonardslee, both towards the western extremity of the Forest Ridges, are other examples of the way in which late 19th-century and 20th-century plantsmen have taken advantage of soil and climate to create gardens of exceptional variety and interest.

The Forest Ridges are well wooded and water flows freely from them. This is an area made by nature for landscape gardening and it is not surprising that it contains two of the most beautiful gardens in the picturesque style, Scotney Castle at Lamberhurst and Sheffield Park on the southern edge of Ashdown Forest, where the Forest Ridges join the Wealden plain.

The chalk Downs, too, though less hospitable to gardeners, have proved a challenge which has resulted in the production of several gardens of outstanding beauty and interest, notably Highdown, made by the late Sir Frederick Stern. This garden is partly situated in a disused chalk quarry in which he was assured by experts that nothing would grow.

The moat and ruins at Scotney Castle

24

Bateman's

Burwash, Sussex. Half-a-mile south of Burwash off the A265 from Cross-in-Hand to Hawkhurst. The National Trust. Open daily except Fridays (but on Good Friday), from early March to late October.

The substantial stone-built Jacobean house is famous as the home, for many years, of Rudyard Kipling. It is a lovely building and the garden, without being in any way spectacular, makes a dignified setting for it. There are wide lawns at different levels, good clipped hedges of yew, and walls of Sussex sandstone matching the walls of the building itself. Two fine lines of pleached lime trees are centred on the south side of the house and a large rectangular pond, originally made as a bathing pool for the Kipling children, but carefully designed and placed so that it adds materially to the attractiveness of the garden. At one end of the pool is a paved rose garden, at the other a seat backed by low walls of Sussex stone and a clipped yew hedge. Beyond these formal gardens flows the Dudwell, here a steep-banked trout stream, and a path leads for some distance beside this, flanked by many good trees and shrubs.

Bedgebury Pinetum

Goudhurst, Kent. Two-and-a-half miles south of Goudhurst on the B2079 to Flimwell. The Forestry Commission. Open daily throughout the year.

The National Pinetum at Bedgebury is an extension of the Royal Botanic Gardens, Kew, and was started in 1925 when it became apparent that soil and atmospheric conditions at Kew would make it impossible to grow many coniferous trees satisfactorily there. It is, therefore, primarily a scientific collection, but it has been planted with so much skill, and it occupies a site of such great natural beauty, that it is a delight to the eye, appreciated by anyone who enjoys woodland gardens.

The 64-acre pinetum occupies two small valleys and the sharp ridge of land between them. Small streams flow through each of these valleys and where they meet a considerable lake has been formed by damming. For convenience of scientific work the various conifers have been grouped according to their families, but the density of planting has been varied from one part to another, many open glades have been left, and wide rides or avenues intersect the plantations and provide

The pool and rose garden at Bateman's, backed by pleached lime trees. This garden was made by Rudyard Kipling, who lived there for many years

many delightful vistas. Moreover, although this is a pinetum, ostensibly devoted exclusively to coniferous trees, numerous rhododendrons and broad-leaved trees have been included for variety and pictorial effect, so much so that the approach to the pinetum from the car park is through an avenue of sweet gums (liquidambar) and down a bank which is also planted with birch species and ornamental cherries. This leads to one of the largest avenues in the pinetum, Dallimore Avenue, running right through the western valley to Marshall's Lake and the plantation of swamp cypress (taxodium) and dawn redwood (metasequoia) beside it. Another avenue leads over the hill past the collections of junipers, cedars, larches, etc. and so down into the eastern valley where there is an especially beautiful grove of cypresses (cupressus and chamaecyparis). On the far side of this valley yews, in a great variety of shapes and colours, are planted and an open glade leads to Pine Hill and so out of the pinetum to footpaths to Cranbrook and Flimwell.

Though the planning of the pinetum is, in general, completely informal there is one touch of formality on the summit of the ridge: a short avenue flanked by some of the finest specimens of Leyland Cypress (*Cupressocyparis leylandii*) in the country.

Borde Hill

Haywards Heath, Sussex. One-and-a-half miles north of Haywards Heath on the more easterly of the two roads to Balcombe. Privately owned. Open on Sundays and Wednesdays from late March to late August and on Sundays only in September.

This fine garden, mainly planted in the woodland and glade manner, is pleasantly sited on a saddle of land with extensive views, particularly to the north. There are also two large dells, possibly the site of mineral workings in earlier times, which have provided the garden makers with further variations in contour. Full use has been taken of this to convert the larger dell into a kind of tropical jungle of rhododendrons and other exotic shrubs, and the smaller dell into a water and foliage garden with a small pool and luxuriant plantings of ferns, hostas, astilbes, irises and other plants.

On the ridge of land between these dells and the house is one of the few semi-formal features in the garden, an area of raised rectangular beds so heavily planted with anthemis and other perennials that its architectural qualities are largely concealed. All around is thin woodland thickly underplanted with rhododendrons,

azaleas, magnolias, camellias and other shrubs, the whole pleasantly contrasted with an open lawn behind the house, flanked by more beds of azaleas, but open to the south to reveal the Sussex farmland which makes so beautiful a background.

The north front of the house has a stone-balustraded terrace commanding the most extensive views of the countryside over a little garden of island beds set in grass, the planting again being predominantly of rhododendrons. Still more plantings of these shrubs are to be found in two of the woodlands to the north-east, but these have not been so highly developed nor maintained at so good a level of cultivation as in the main garden around the house.

Above. Azaleas growing beside the lawn at Borde Hill

Below. Swamp cypresses growing beside the lake in Bedgebury Pinetum

Chartwell

Westerham, Kent. Two miles south of Westerham off the B2026 to Edenbridge. The National Trust. Open on Sundays, Wednesdays, Thursdays, Saturdays and Bank Holiday Mondays from April to mid-October.

Chartwell is famous as having been for many years the home of Sir Winston Churchill. The house is old and has seen many changes and additions, but the garden as it is to-day is very largely the creation of Sir Winston. His love of water is to be seen in the series of pools, waterfalls and cascades in the open landscape to the north of the house; the water rushing downhill in a torrent to fill a large circular swimming pool and then discharging into the twin lakes which fill the lower part of the valley on the west side of which the house stands. One of the larger pools, almost completely encircled by bamboos, contains Sir Winston's famous golden orfe which he loved to watch. This part of the garden must have been especially dear to him as several of his paintings show the swimming pool and valley.

The land immediately around the house has been terraced and contains a walled rose garden, a vine-covered pergola leading to the Marlborough Pavilion and, to the south of the house, two grass areas at different levels, one used as a croquet lawn. From these, and from the raised walk which leads from the croquet lawn to what was once the kitchen garden, some of the finest views of the Weald can be obtained. The kitchen garden itself, surrounded by the high brick wall which Sir Winston built with his own hands, is now an ornamental garden with lawns bisected by a flagged path and twin borders planted with yellow roses and set off by catmint and other blue-flowered or grey-leaved perennials. These borders were a gift to Sir Winston and Lady Churchill from their children to commemorate their Golden Wedding.

The Chartwell gardens are all supremely English in character, quiet, well proportioned and dignified, neither over coloured with flowers nor over elaborated with architectural detail.

Crittenden House

Matfield, Kent. Five miles north-east of Royal Tunbridge Wells on the by-road linking the B2015 with the B2160 at Matfield. Privately owned. Open on most Sundays from April to the end of July and on occasional Saturdays.

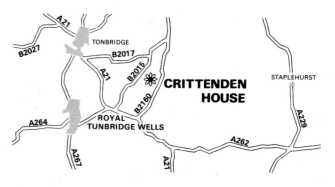

This comparatively small garden (it covers about 4 acres), made in what was once an orchard and still retains many apple trees, is a particularly beautiful example of island beds informally disposed and permanently planted with shrubs and herbaceous perennials, used to create a very colourful garden which does not require a great deal of upkeep and which fits naturally into the landscape. The house is typical of many Kentish farmhouses, which once it was, and the large pond near it has been converted into a fine water garden. There are two other pools situated in deep depressions which were probably once iron-ore workings, and these, too, have been well planted with moisture-loving plants in and near the water, and with a variety of shrubs and hardy perennials on the steep banks. Large blocks of local sandstone have been used to create a natural-looking cascade and further blocks of the same stone embedded in the turf continue the impression that they belong to the site.

Near the house a more symmetrical style has been adopted with flag-stoned paths, rectangular beds, stone seats and small figures of cherubs. Here there is a rose garden, but the whole planting is so luxuriant and care-free that there is little impression of formality, but rather of a glorified cottage garden with unusually fine and beautiful plants.

28

Charleston Manor

Westdean, Sussex. Three miles north-east of Seaford on the by-road which links the A259 and the A27 from Exceat to Wilmington. Privately owned. Open Monday to Friday mid-May to September.

Opposite top. The vine-covered pergola, Chartwell

Opposite bottom. Sir Winston Churchill's main fish pool

Above. The orchard garden of Crittenden House is cleverly blended with the surrounding countryside

Below. Roses in the cottage garden, Charleston Manor

The flint-built house and its adjacent buildings, including an ancient circular dovecot, a huge tithe barn, now converted into a theatre, and a range of farm sheds disguised as a cottage, lie in a deep fold in the South Downs, and so the garden is made on almost pure chalk. Part, in front of the mock cottage, is enclosed by walls and has twin borders of perennial plants which channel long vistas to the courtyard of the house in one direction and to an old walled orchard in the other.

On the far side of the house, where the tithe barn fills in the bottom of the slope, the ground has been terraced, and buttressed hedges of yew emphasise the firm outline of the design. But the real glory of Charleston Manor garden is its roses, mainly shrub and old-fashioned varieties and climbers, which cover the face of the cottage, scramble up into ancient trees in the orchard (or are supported by pole pyramids where the trees have finally collapsed), and are trained over every available wall. Irises are grown too, as well as helianthemums and other plants that thrive on the chalk, and on the far hillside there is thick woodland which makes a handsome backdrop to the whole scene.

Great Dixter

Northiam, Sussex. Half-a-mile north of Northiam on the A28. Privately owned. Open daily except Monday, but on Bank Holidays, from mid-April to the end of September.

The beautiful half-timbered 15th-century house is of great interest as an outstanding example of restoration and enlargement by Sir Edwin Lutyens about 1910, and he also designed the main framework of the garden. This is divided into several separate sections, some enclosed, almost secret, and formal, others open and informal and with a variety of planting to suit this variety of character. The house is approached by a simple flagged path through a little orchard of walnuts and crab apples growing in rough grass heavily under-planted with bulbs, including fritillaries. To the right is a large sunken garden with an octagonal water-lily pool and surrounding raised borders retained by dry walls. The planting is rich and varied with both per-manent and temporary plants, and two oast houses make a picturesque background. Next there is an entirely enclosed garden in which many varieties of clematis grow on the high walls.

From this, an archway leads to the south side of the house where the land falls away, affording an excellent opportunity for terracing. Elaborate brick steps, designed in a series of circles, lead to the lower level.

One quite large area has been devoted to topiary specimens cut in yew and displayed in mown grass. They are already very large and it is difficult to compre-hend that they have all been planted since 1910. There are also two very large mulberry trees which are genuine antiques.

However, the major glory of the gardens at Great Dixter is the Long Border beyond these mulberries. It is 70 yards long and 5 yards wide and is backed by a yew hedge and bounded in front by a wide flagged path. This border has been planned and planted with shrubs, climbers, herbaceous perennials and dahlias to give a fine display over an exceptionally long season. Facing it is an orchard with naturalised bulbs, and there is also a formal yew-enclosed rose garden backed by a thatched outhouse. Other features include a small garden of old-fashioned flowers and another one planted with lavender.

Two views in the gardens of Great Dixter. Above is the sunken garden with its octagonal pool and a background of oast houses ; and below, the famous Long Border in which trees, shrubs, climbers, herbaceous plants and dahlias are combined with great skill

Highdown Gardens

Goring, Sussex. One mile north of Ferring on the A259 from Goring to Littlehampton. Worthing Corporation. Open Monday to Friday throughout the year, and on the first Sundays in July, August and September. Also open on Good Friday and Bank Holidays.

The great interest in this garden is that it has been made on a chalk hillside and in a disused chalk quarry and that, despite the apparently unfavourable character of the soil, it contains a very fine collection of plants. These range from daffodils and anemones to fine trees such as the Indian chestnut *(Aesculus indica)* and the handkerchief tree (davidia). The whole face of the chalk quarry, once bare, has been covered with ivies, conifers and other vegetation, and in the quarry itself two pools have been made, one surrounded by a rock garden and the other by bamboos, primulas and other moisture-loving plants. The plan is, in the main, informal and good use has been made of the irregular contours of the site to increase the sense of size and variety. Paths wind through it, now entering open glades, now plunging into areas of dense planting, and continually bringing fresh delights to view.

But this was also a garden to which a great plantsman, the late Sir Frederick Stern, brought plants from many parts of the world and carried out his own experiments in plant breeding. To accommodate many of these he made long beds, separated by grass walks, on the more open parts of the hillside, where plants could easily be cared for and observed. Many of the roses, daffodils, peonies, irises, fox-tail lilies (eremurus) and other plants he raised continue to thrive in these beds and provide a living catalogue of what will grow on a thin chalk soil.

The steep drive leading to the house is flanked by daffodils which make an impressive display in spring, and from the forecourt there are fine views of the coast.

Above is the rose garden and sundial at the entrance to Highdown Gardens; and below, a spring scene in the garden with wide grass walks between beds informally planted with daffodils and exotic trees and shrubs

Penshurst Place

Penshurst, Kent. At Penshurst, four miles south-west of Tonbridge on the B2176 to Chiddingstone Causeway, from the A26. Privately owned. Open on Thursdays, Saturdays and Sundays during April and May, and open daily, except for Mondays and Fridays, from June to September.

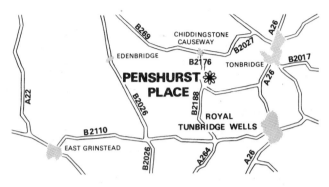

Penshurst Place is one of the best preserved mediaeval mansions in England. Its Great Hall was built about 1340 and no part of it is later than early 17th century. It is fortunate that its garden matches it in dignity, having been restored in the mid-19th century to something resembling its 16th-century character. Topiary plays a prominent part, but not in any fanciful forms. There is a long, yew-enclosed alley cutting through the garden with various more open spaces along its length, including one almost completely filled by a rectangular pool of water.

In front of the house is a parterre with a raised terrace on two sides from which it can be viewed. The design is simple, the beds either being edged with box and planted with roses, or filled with box cut in flat-topped moulded slabs, as though carved out of green stone. The centre-piece is a circular water basin with a statue surrounded by jets.

There are other less formal features, one of the most charming being the use of apple trees in little plantations, divided by trim hedges and flanked by borders of perennial flowers. There is a homely atmosphere about this entirely in keeping with the Kentish countryside which Penshurst Place graces so well.

Below. The parterre at Penshurst Place, in which some beds are planted with roses and others are filled with box, trimmed in solid patterned slabs

Above. This unusual sundial, surrounded by a dahlia-filled bed, terminates the long, yew-enclosed alley which cuts through the garden at Penshurst Place

Sissinghurst Castle

Sissinghurst, Kent. Two-and-a-half miles north-east of Cranbrook on the A262 from Goudhurst to Biddenden. The National Trust. Open daily from April to October.

The slender twin towers of Sissinghurst Castle, looking from a little distance so like a set for a romantic film, were obviously never intended for war. It is, therefore, no surprise to learn that they belonged, not to a real castle, but to an Elizabethan mansion, much of which has long since disappeared. Indeed, when in 1930 the late Victoria Sackville-West and her husband the late Sir Harold Nicholson purchased the property, the whole of it was derelict and there was no vestige of a garden. It was through their combined genius that the buildings were restored and provided with gardens to match them in refinement and beauty. For, though the total area of land at Sissinghurst is not great, it has been divided into a number of separate gardens each with a character of its own, but all linked together so cunningly that there is complete unity in the whole design.

There are points of similarity with Hidcote Manor (see p. 84), notably in the long walks passing through the gardens and linking them together. There is a similar contrast of open spaces with areas less densely planted, and the same careful association of colours, here a blue border, there a white and silver garden, elsewhere one planted mainly with yellow and orange flowers. Throughout, though the design is firm and even formal, the planting softens the lines and gives the whole a rustic luxuriance. Yet Sissinghurst is in no way a copy of Hidcote. Similar methods are applied in quite different ways. The castle is central to the design, which Hidcote Manor is not, and the two adjacent buildings, one a cottage, the other a priest's house, are closely integrated with it.

Old roses play a much more important part at Sissinghurst, nearly filling the largest of the gardens and spilling over into most of the others. There is an avenue of pleached limes, leading to a nuttery, and both are underplanted in highly original ways, the lime avenue with flanking carpets of small spring-flowering plants, including bulbs and alpines, the nut bushes with a dense cover of polyanthuses. Beyond the nuttery is a charming herb garden, and from this point the old moat wraps around a large orchard which has been heavily underplanted with daffodils and in which the branches of many of the trees are weighed down with climbing roses.

Most of the planting is permanent, with hardy perennials, shrubs, roses and trees, but every kind of plant is welcome at Sissinghurst if it serves a desired purpose. And in the broadest terms that purpose is to keep the gardens beautiful throughout the year.

A flower-filled urn in one of several enclosed gardens at Sissinghurst Castle, each arranged as a delightful surprise for the visitor

Another of the little gardens, with the twin towers of Sissinghurst Castle in the background. This one is planted mainly in shades of yellow and orange

Hever Castle

Hever, Kent. Two miles south-east of Edenbridge off the B2026 to Hartfield. Privately owned. Open on Sundays and Wednesdays from Easter to the end of September, also on Saturdays in August and September.

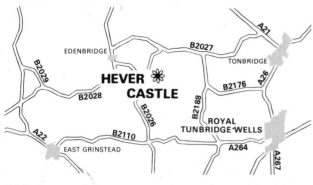

This is one of the most popular gardens with visitors, partly because of the romantic appearance of the little castle, the birthplace of Anne Boleyn and for some years the home of Anne of Cleves, and partly because of the highly unusual garden created by the first Viscount Astor after he purchased the property in 1903. Lord Astor, before he became a British citizen, had been American Minister in Rome and had made a considerable collection of ancient sculpture. To accommodate this and objects of archaeological interest, he made a large garden in the Italian manner at some distance from the castle, enclosed by walls, a colonnaded pergola and, at the east end, a magnificent piazza with stone steps leading to a 35-acre lake which was excavated to complete this ambitious conception. Other notable features of the Hever Castle gardens are a half-moon pool presided over by a marble statue of Venus, at the west end of the Italian garden; a walled rose garden with more of Lord Astor's Roman sculp-

ture; a very long herbaceous border; a large rock garden planted with herbaceous plants rather than alpines, and, between the original moat of the castle and a second larger moat which Lord Astor made outside it, a maze and a series of small enclosed gardens one of which contains a remarkable set of giant chessmen cut out of golden yew. Water-lilies thrive in the moats, topiary specimens decorate the lawns in front of the castle, daffodils in thousands are naturalised in the rougher grass and there are a great many fine trees and rare plants throughout the garden.

Two features at Hever Castle. Above is the Rotunda on the south side of the Italian garden, with a Roman statue of a youth; and below, a view across the outer of the two moats to the castle

Leonardslee

Lower Beeding, Sussex. Four-and-a-half miles south-east of Horsham on the A281 to Cowfold. Privately owned. Open on Sundays, Wednesdays, Thursdays and Saturdays throughout May.

This is one of the very great woodland gardens of the late 19th and early 20th century. Sir Edmund Loder began planting in 1888 and the work has been continued by his descendants to the present day. The garden occupies about 100 acres on both sides of a large and well-wooded valley in St Leonard's Forest, and makes use of a chain of old hammer ponds in the valley, fed by a stream flowing through it. Into this naturally beautiful setting has been brought a great collection of the finest exotic trees and shrubs, in particular rhododendrons, azaleas, camellias and magnolias. Many of the rhododendrons are hybrids created at Leonardslee and the original bushes of the most famous of these, *Rhododendron loderi*, planted in

One of the old hammer ponds at Leonardslee. The well-wooded valley sides have been heavily underplanted with rhododendrons, azaleas and other exotic trees and shrubs, which create a jungle-like profusion

1903, are still there, now over 20 feet high and laden with huge white or pink fragrant flowers each May.

The house stands on the lip of the valley facing west. A lawn laps around it, itself partly encircled by rhododendrons and other shrubs. From this lawn there are views to the South Downs, 10 miles distant, as well as down into the valley immediately below. A wide gravelled walk separates the lawn from a rock garden, and is known variously as the Camellia Walk or the Palm Walk since so many specimens of each grow beside it. The palms regularly regenerate themselves by self-sown seed. The rock garden has the appearance of a small ravine, and is planted principally with evergreen azaleas in a variety of colours.

For the rest, the plan of this jungle garden is completely informal. Paths lead through the woods which are thickly underplanted with rhododendrons and azaleas. In the valley a wide path runs from end to end, skirting the lakes and providing some of the most splendid views of the colour on the valley sides and the reflections in the water. Mossy Gill, across the valley, is filled with yellow-flowered azaleas, the most spicily fragrant of all. There are ornamental cherries, magnolias, snowdrop trees (halesia) and many other rare or beautiful specimens, but, above all, it is the luxuriance and the brilliance of the rhododendrons which astounds and delights visitors to this highly popular and delightful garden.

Nymans

Handcross, Surrey. Four-and-a-half miles south of Crawley off the A23 to Brighton. The National Trust. Open on Tuesdays, Wednesdays, Thursdays, Saturdays, Sundays and Bank Holiday Mondays from April to late October.

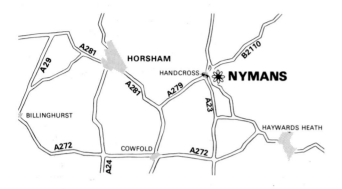

Garden making began at Nymans towards the close of the 19th century and was continued by three generations of a family keenly interested in plants and highly gifted in the art of garden making. There is no strong central design but rather a series of gardens each, to a considerable degree, self-contained yet happily and unobtrusively linked together.

The most open part is a meadow, the park, to the north-east of the house, sloping steeply to the woods below. This is heavily underplanted with daffodils and is flanked by the pinetum, now somewhat overgrown, but still with many magnificent specimens of rare trees. The heather garden, with its labyrinth of narrow paths winding between rocky banks, now almost completely covered by a dense growth of heathers and other shrubs, gives the greatest feeling of enclosure. It is a natural descendant of the wilderness of older gardens, but is far more interesting because of the quality of the planting.

The strongest element of formality is seen in the forecourt, with its high hedges of yew, stone walls and pavilion, and in the Wall Garden where broad paths set at right angles meet at a stone fountain surrounded by four very large and quite elaborately clipped yews. The paths are flanked by wide borders of hardy plants and bulbs backed by shrubs, and there are plants of clematis trained up pear-shaped wire supports in a manner of which Miss Jekyll doubtless approved and may even have suggested. Similar thoughts may cross the visitor's mind on seeing the beds of roses and hydrangeas on the great shrub-enclosed lawn, the roses enclosed in a surround of trained ivy, the hydrangeas in a kind of rambler rose basket with cross-over handles of winter jasmine. There are many other delightful features at Nymans, including a long wisteria-covered pergola and an overflow garden across the road, made to accommodate the flood of new plants which swamped so many British gardens in the first half of the present century.

Below left. The lawns at Nymans looking towards the forecourt with kniphofias in the foreground

Below right. Summer-flowering shrubs in the Wall Garden at Nymans. Beyond is the stone pavilion capped by a dovecot and backed by the house

Sheffield Park

Sheffield Green, Sussex. Six-and-a-half miles south of Forest Row on the A275 to Lewes. The National Trust. Open daily from May to October inclusive, and on Wednesdays, Saturdays, Sundays and Bank Holidays in April.

This is a supreme example of a landscape garden which has been used by later generations for a large collection of exotic trees and shrubs, for so successfully has the operation been done, that it is difficult to imagine that the garden as it exists to-day was not so conceived from the outset. The house is a castellated mansion in the neo-Gothic style built in the late 18th century and standing at the head of a broad shallow valley. The original landscaping was carried out by Lancelot Brown who created two lakes by damming a stream flowing through a second valley at right angles to the first. Doubtless he planted clumps of native trees to channel the view to the water and the surrounding country, but no plans exist and so this must remain a surmise.

Nothing further appears to have been done until the last quarter of the 19th century when the 3rd Lord Sheffield created two further lakes, this time in the upper valley, thereby creating a huge inverted T of water centred on the house. There was a considerable drop in level between the first and second lakes and here he built a waterfall and flanking rock garden. He also constructed a stone-balustraded bridge on the dam between the lakes from which some of the most beautiful views are to be obtained. Lord Sheffield added to the planting with exotic trees and shrubs, notably some columnar conifers and great masses of rhododendrons.

The final transformation from 18th-century to 20th-century ideas of landscape gardening occurred between 1909 and 1934 when the property was owned by the late Mr Arthur Soames. He not only planted an impressive collection of trees and shrubs, but also raised hundreds of rhododendrons from his own crosses and purchased many more of the best hybrid rhododendrons then available. He also planted great numbers of bulbs, including bluebells which by some chance did not grow wild here in any quantity. All these he disposed around the four great lakes and in the groves and walks which he created in the 60 acres or so of land contained between them. Many of the trees and shrubs he chose primarily for their autumn foliage, placing them where they would be reflected in the lakes, so that Sheffield Park gardens are as justly famous for their late colour as for their spring display.

An autumn scene at Sheffield Park when the rich colours of the trees are given an added beauty by being reflected in one or other of the several lakes

Scotney Castle

Lamberhurst, Kent. Half-a-mile south of Lamberhurst on the A21 from Royal Tunbridge Wells to Hastings. Privately owned. Open on Wednesdays, Saturdays and Bank Holidays from Easter Saturday to the end of October, and on Sundays in October.

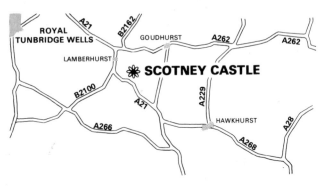

Like Stourhead (see p. 50) nearly a hundred years earlier, the garden at Scotney Castle was the work of a gifted amateur and is a supremely beautiful example of its own style, the 'picturesque'. The creator, Mr Edward Hussey, was strongly influenced by the ideas of the Rev. W. Gilpin, Uvedale Price and Payne Knight and he employed William Sawry Gilpin, a nephew of the Rev. Gilpin, as an advisor. Moreover, he had at his disposal an ideal site, a deep, well-wooded valley in which was a moated building of highly romantic appearance, which had started as a mediaeval castle and grown into a small mansion as a result of numerous additions and alterations, the two most important of which had been made about 1580 and 1630. As Mr Hussey was about to build a new house for himself on higher ground, he carefully chose the site to command the finest possible view of these old buildings, and further enhanced the dramatic possibilities by quarrying the stone for his home immediately below this site. This he terraced, building a stone-balustraded bastion on the very edge of the quarry, which he converted into a natural rock garden, now filled with azaleas and other shrubs and colourful plants, over which to view the valley below. It only remained to dismantle a considerable part of the 17th-century portion of the old building to provide an authentic ruin to form the centre-piece of his essay in landscaping.

The details were filled in with as much care as the broad outlines of the scheme. Broad-leaved trees and conifers – some strongly columnar in habit, some, such as the Lebanon cedar on the slope beyond the ruins, flat and spreading – were placed to produce the maximum dramatic effect. Great masses of rhododendrons, kalmias and other shrubs were planted on the near slope to fill in the foreground and the native trees did the rest.

Succeeding generations have lovingly cared for Mr Hussey's creation and have added to it in ways that he would have approved. As a result it is an extremely beautiful garden.

Scenes in the garden at Scotney Castle. At the top is the 17th-century house, partially dismantled to make a romantic ruin. In the middle is the view of the picturesque landscape from the balustraded bastion above the quarry from which the stone for the new house was excavated. At the bottom is the reverse view from the ruins to the 19th-century house

38

Wakehurst Place

Ardingly, Sussex. One mile north of Ardingly on the B2028 from Haywards Heath to Turner's Hill. The National Trust. Administered by the Royal Botanic Gardens, Kew. Open daily throughout the year, except Christmas Day.

To accommodate his plants he adopted two major styles of gardening; in the upper parts around the house and rock garden, a kind of open glade planting with long island beds of varying shape and size separated by areas of grass; and further afield on the slopes of the valley, woodland gardening consisting very largely of infilling the existing woodland with exotic trees and shrubs. The style becomes progressively more natural and even wild the further one progresses. There is an extensive pinetum and a good heather garden. Flower colour is at its maximum in late spring and early summer and there is very fine foliage colour in the autumn. Since the garden came under the control of Kew there has been a tendency to diversify the planting still further and so increase the botanical character of the garden, and at the same time to widen and improve the paths to give better access; treatment which has given the garden a slightly more park-like appearance.

This is one of the great British plant collections, and it is also a very lovely garden. Situated on a ridge of high land running north and south, the steep-sided valleys on each side drain away cold air and make the garden relatively frost free in spring. Wakehurst also has the advantage of a lime-free soil and a great deal of native woodland which provides protection for the more exotic trees and shrubs.

Much of the planting, which has made the garden world famous, was carried out between 1903 and 1938 by Mr Gerald W. E. Loder, who later became Lord Wakehurst. During this period he constantly extended the garden and stocked it with a great variety of plants including rhododendrons, azaleas, magnolias, camellias and maples. He made a large rock garden beside the upper lake and used other lakes further afield for moisture-loving plants.

Two scenes at Wakehurst Place. Below, the house is seen through massed plantings of maples and azaleas. At the foot of the page the house as seen from another point, across the rock garden lake, with an arbour cut out of yew on the far bank

The South

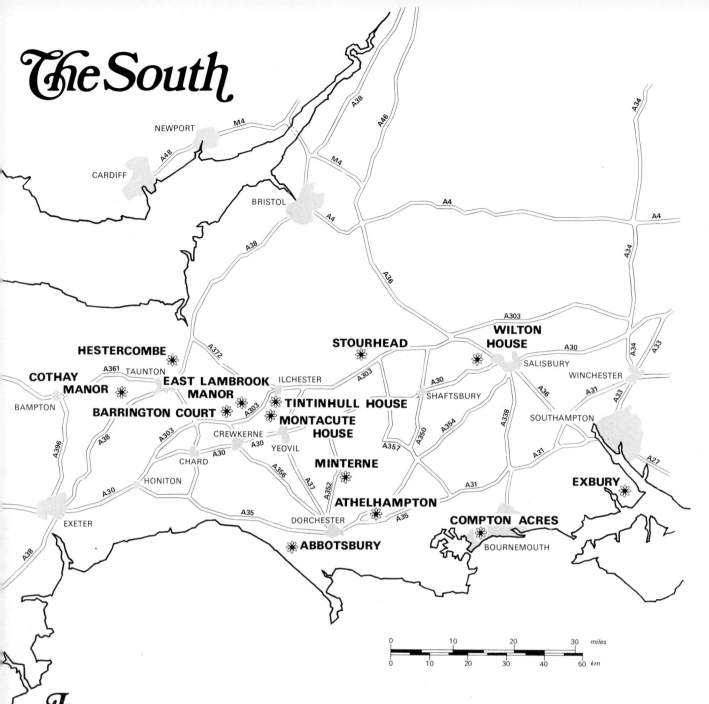

I am very conscious that 'The South' is a vague description which needs definition. For the purpose of this book I shall do this by stating that it includes the whole of Hampshire, Dorset and Wiltshire as well as the eastern half of Somerset.

It is bounded on the north by the vast area of Salisbury Plain, for the most part too bleak in climate and harsh in soil to encourage the finest garden making. But it also includes many far more favourable areas: the New Forest in the south where the soil is sandy or peaty and rhododendrons grow like weeds, and the lovely rolling country south of the Mendip Hills where the soil changes every few miles, and the valleys with their streams are an invitation to experiment with plants and designs. The greatest experiment of all, and one that proved triumphantly successful, was that of Henry Hoare, in the middle of the 18th century, when he built a dam across one of these valleys, so

creating a roughly triangular lake around which he erected a succession of delightful classical temples and other buildings and planted the valley sides with beech and fir. Later generations have varied and enriched the planting and Stourhead is to-day one of the most beautiful landscape gardens in the country.

This mild southern part of England, with its comparatively easy access to Bristol, Southampton and London, has attracted men of wealth for centuries and great houses abound in it. Montacute, Athelhampton and Barrington Court are just three of the many examples of very old and beautiful houses in this area, and each has a garden to suit its character, though some have only been made in modern times.

Naturalised daffodils at Barrington Court

40

Abbotsbury

Sub-tropical Gardens, Dorset. One mile from Abbotsbury on the road to the Chesil Beach. Privately owned. Open daily from April to mid-September.

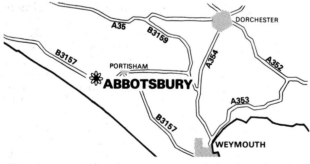

This is one of the famous tree and shrub collections made during the 19th century and it contains a great wealth of plants including many exotic specimens now grown to great size. There are palm trees, dracaenas and acacias as well as great numbers of rhododendrons, azaleas, magnolias, camellias, hydrangeas and many other genera. Little attempt has been made to arrange these to conform with any obvious order or design, and the overall effect is rather of a jungle of growth penetrated by gravelled paths with, here and there, a more open area of grass. In the centre is a rectangular walled garden which must once have contained more formal beds, but, because of the luxuriant growth of the plants in the mild maritime climate, there is now little distinction between what is inside the walls and the woodland around.

Palms and many other tender plants thrive in the mild climate of the Abbotsbury Sub-tropical Gardens, close to the sea by the Chesil Beach, in Dorset

Athelhampton

Puddletown, Dorset. One mile east of Puddletown on the A35 from Dorchester to Poole. Privately owned. Open on Wednesdays and Thursdays from Easter to September, on Sundays from June to September, and also on Bank Holiday Sundays and Mondays and on Good Friday.

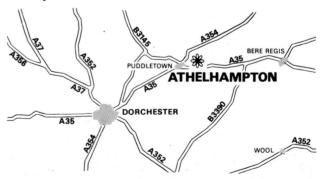

Athelhampton is a very old house, some parts of it having been built in the late 15th century and the whole of it completed before the end of the 16th century. It is built of mellow grey stone and an equally ancient, circular stone dovecot stands beside it.

It is fitting that such a house should have a beautiful garden and, looking at its massive yew hedges, its towering topiary pyramids and its handsome stone terraces and pavilions, one might imagine that they were all contemporary with the house or, at the very least, were centuries old. Yet, in fact, these walled and hedged gardens did not exist before 1891 and the effect of age is due to the skill of the craftsmanship and the use of the same Ham stone as that of which the house is constructed.

There are two large formal gardens separated by two smaller ones arranged on a cross axis, so that long vistas can be obtained through them. The more elaborate of the large gardens is dominated by a high stone terrace flanked by stone pavilions and from this eminence one can look down on the sunken lawn and water-lily pool. Here are the largest clipped yew pyramids and the most massive hedges, but the enclosure is not so complete as to exclude views of the house and of the fine tree planting around.

Each of the other walled gardens has its own character and planting; there are handsome wrought-iron gates, good statues, ornaments and fountains and a pleasant variety in the planting. A river flows behind the house and a path leads beside this to a garden of a quite different style to the west; a large open lawn to display the dovecot, semi-wild planting of shrub roses and moisture-loving plants, a long vista between yew hedges and a secluded walk between well-planted herbaceous borders.

ʙarrington Court

Above. One of the formal gardens at Athelhampton
Below. The walled garden at Barrington Court

Barrington, Somerset. Three miles north-east of Ilminster on the road from Puckington to Shepton Beauchamp. The National Trust. Open every Wednesday throughout the year and on occasional Sundays.

There are two linked houses at Barrington Court, one stone and Tudor the other brick and Caroline, and there are several gardens to match them, though these are entirely 20th-century creations. In some, notably the charming iris garden with clematis trained on wire frames, trimmed box, grey stone sundial and liberal use of lavender, catmint and other grey and blue plants, the ideas of Gertrude Jekyll can be seen.

The largest of the gardens is a rectangle enclosed on three sides by high brick walls, and on the fourth by the south front of the 17th-century building which was originally a stable block but has now been converted for use as a dwelling house. This garden is entirely formal, in keeping with the rather severe architecture. It has a long water-lily pool, and raised rectangular beds, retained by brick walls, and filled with crinums, bedding plants and annuals. The flanking borders are densely planted with herbaceous perennials and shrubs and there are many climbers on the walls.

Another enclosed garden is devoted to roses. Here there are long borders filled with roses as well as a separate herbaceous border sheltered by the kitchen garden wall and faced by a border of floribunda roses. Elsewhere, shrubs are planted informally in large beds of irregular shape separated by grass paths; but around the Tudor house the planting has been kept to a minimum, with wide areas of grass and just a few trees, so that the full beauty of its Gothic architecture can be appreciated.

Compton Acres

Poole, Dorset. On the Canford Cliffs Road between Poole and Bournemouth. Privately owned. Open daily from April (Good Friday if earlier) to October inclusive.

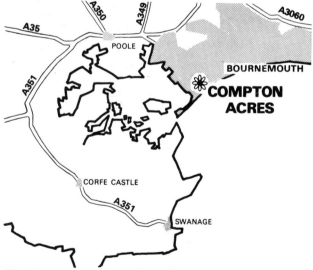

The house, an Edwardian villa, stands on a bluff, of what was once moorland, overlooking Poole harbour, and the gardens which encircle it were made during the 1920s. There are eight of them in all, each representing a different style, and, since little attempt has been made to integrate them, the effect is rather that of an orderly and extremely well-maintained series of exhibitions, linked but each entire in itself.

Centrally placed in front of the house, and commanding the finest views, is an 'English' garden complete with croquet lawn, rose beds, flower borders and reproductions of 18th-century statues of shepherds and shepherdesses. The other seven gardens, starting from the entrance gates and proceeding in a clockwise manner, are a little paved patio garden said to be Roman in style; twin borders leading to an Italian garden; a long and narrow Palm Court; a very large rock garden overlooking a wild garden in the chine below; a heather garden and finally a Japanese garden. Of these, the Italian and Japanese gardens are the most ambitious. The former contains a water-lily pool in the form of a very elongated cross with an elaborate fountain in the centre, and bronze statues of wrestlers at one end. It is overlooked by a stone-balustraded terrace, has a small domed temple at the far end and is lavishly planted with flowers in season.

The Japanese garden is really a large rock and water garden with Japanese statues, ornaments and buildings including a red Tea House and a bronze archway, or Torre Gate, with ascending and descending dragons, and many Japanese maples.

Above. The richly-planted Italian Garden at Compton Acres, with long pool, temple, elaborate fountain and bronze figures of the Wrestlers of Herculaneum

Opposite top. The water-lily pool and fountain at Cothay Manor, surrounded by simple topiary specimens

Opposite bottom. One of the lakes at Exbury in the woodland filled with azaleas, rhododendrons, Japanese maples and many other exotic trees and shrubs

Cothay Manor

Greenham, Somerset. Four miles west of Wellington off the A38 to Exeter. Privately owned. Open on Spring and Late Summer Bank Holiday Sundays and Mondays, on Thursdays and each first Sunday from June to early September and also on Wednesdays in August.

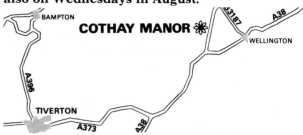

This beautiful stone-built house of the late 15th century is remotely situated down narrow lanes and is almost encircled by water, with the River Tone flowing through the meadows to the west and a brook feeding a large pond to the east. The garden lies between house and river, a wide rectangle extending the long line of the house itself. This characteristic has been accentuated by making a yew alley bisect the garden lengthwise, with the exception of one central area where a cross axis from the house permits views over a sunken garden, and, through a wrought-iron gate, to the meadows and river beyond.

From this central alleyway, yew-buttressed openings give access to a series of intimate gardens, one devoted to roses, another to irises, a third almost completely filled by a rectangular pool. The sunken garden is treated as a little parterre, with patterned beds edged with box accented with a ring of topiary specimens and planted with roses and other flowers. The result is a a garden as secluded as the house itself, and completely in character with it, though much is of fairly recent construction. Visitors will go to Cothay Manor primarily to see the house, but none should miss this very English garden.

Exbury

Exbury, Hampshire. Three miles south-east of Beaulieu off the B3054 at Hill Top. Privately owned. Open daily, except Saturdays, from mid-April to early June.

This is a woodland garden of almost unexampled size and splendour. It covers about 250 acres and contains the immense collection of rhododendron species and hybrids made by the late Mr Lionel de Rothschild as well as a great many other fine shrubs and trees. It is placed where the New Forest adjoins the Solent, in country naturally well wooded and highly suitable for the cultivation of these plants, many of which have grown to great size. They are arranged in a natural manner as undergrowth in the woodland and around several lakes. Some very long and wide avenues have been left through the wood to provide vistas, and narrower paths provide access to other parts.

The Exbury azaleas are particularly famous for their wide range of colours and the size and quality of the flowers, and since many of these are grouped in very large drifts they add greatly to the brilliance of this remarkable garden in spring and early summer. Daffodils, naturalised in the grass, further add to the spring display making an unforgettable sight in this very lovely garden.

45

Montacute House

Montacute, Somerset. Three miles west of Yeovil on the B3088 towards Ilminster. The National Trust. Open daily, except Mondays and Tuesdays (but on Bank Holiday Mondays), from Easter Saturday to the end of September. Open on Wednesdays, Saturdays and Sundays from March to Easter and in October and November.

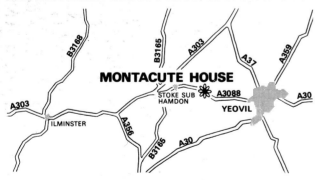

Montacute House and its forecourt are near perfect examples of the taste and craftsmanship of the late 16th century. The forecourt is flanked by elegant pavilions built of the same local Ham stone as the house itself, and the stone balustrading which surrounds it is further ornamented with little obelisks and slender stone lanterns.

The entrance to Montacute House is no longer through this forecourt, but by a straight drive from the road on the opposite side of the building. Therefore, during the 19th century, the old forecourt was transformed into a garden with two other large rectangles, that to the

north on the site of an original Elizabethan garden, that to the south in what was once an orchard. The three not only fit together supremely well, but also perfectly complement the building. Perhaps the most remarkable factor is the quality of the stonework around the formal lily pool and fountain which is the central feature in the north garden, for this matches the stonework of the original forecourt and already looks as old, though it was not made until the 1890s. In the south garden is a conservatory also built in the same 16th-century style.

All these gardens have been planted with great skill and restraint, the late Victoria Sackville-West having had much to do with the selection of suitable plants.

Tintinhull House

Tintinhull, Somerset. Two-and-a-half miles south-west of Ilchester off the A303 to Ilminster. The National Trust. Open on Wednesdays, Thursdays, Saturdays and Bank Holiday Mondays from April to October.

Tintinhull House would be a pleasant but unremarkable early 17th-century building were it not for the beautiful Queen Anne facade in Ham stone which was added to it later. This completely transformed its west front and, in the present century, it has been given a garden which fits it perfectly. The garden is, moreover, a fine example of how to obtain a great deal of variety from a comparatively small area and yet, at the same time, to increase the impression of size.

This has been achieved by centring a wide flagged path on the house and extending it the whole length of the garden westwards, but dividing the area around it into three sections with walls and hedges which project from each side like the wings of a stage. Cones of clipped box line the path, further accentuating its length and concealing the little gardens through which it passes. Each of these is different in character, that at the far end containing a circular lily pool and fountain as a focal point. Two more gardens are on the north side of this main axis; one with a long rectangular pool overlooked by a garden room, the other almost square and dominated by an old Lebanon cedar and a very large yew. The pool garden is centred on the middle section of the long walk so providing an impressive cross view from it.

Throughout, the planting is mainly with permanent plants, herbaceous perennials and shrubs being interwoven with great skill and a highly sensitive regard for colour combinations. In consequence, this is a garden from which any potential garden maker can learn many useful lessons, even in the planning and planting of the tiny gardens which are usual in modern small properties.

Opposite top. The formal gardens at Montacute House are a 19th-century development in a 16th-century setting and perfectly complement the building

Opposite bottom. One of the Elizabethan stone pavilions in the forecourt garden at Montacute House

The long vista at Tintinhull House as seen from the water-lily pool at the far end, towards the Queen Anne façade, through three intimate gardens

East Lambrook Manor

East Lambrook, Somerset. Four miles north-east of Ilminster on the road from Puckington (B3168) to Stapleton (B3165). Privately owned. Due to the death of the owner, Mrs Margery Fish, future opening dates are not known at the time of going to press.

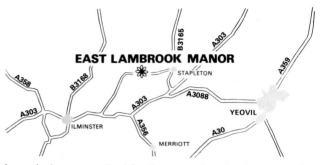

EAST LAMBROOK MANOR

The attractive stone-built manor house is quite small, and dates from both the 15th and the 17th centuries. It stands right in the village of East Lambrook and the garden, no more than an acre in extent, is of considerable interest, partly because of the many rare or unusual hardy plants which it contains, and partly from the skill with which they have been arranged in so small a place. There is a curving lawn to display the house and give a sense of space; the rest of the garden is entirely covered with plants, rather in the style of a traditional cottage garden, but great care has been used in the association of plants to secure the best colour effects and ensure continuity of bloom. Full use has been made of foliage plants and also of ground cover to suppress weeds and reduce labour and cost of upkeep, essential factors for many gardeners.

Minterne

Minterne Magna, Dorset. Two miles north of Cerne Abbas on the A352 from Dorchester to Sherborne. Privately owned. Open on Sundays and Bank Holidays from April to June inclusive.

Minterne stands high above the little River Cerne and its garden has been made on the steep side of the valley and in the water-meadows below. It is a site ready-made for a wild woodland garden of the type which became so popular early in the present century, and full advantage has been taken of its natural qualities. The effect, now that the trees and shrubs have reached maturity, is of a jungle-like profusion.

The main path leads down into the valley, follows a horse-shoe bend around a spur, which provides a natural stage for many rhododendrons, azaleas and other exotic shrubs, and finally returns to the house. Minor paths lead away over little bridges and across stepping stones to the moister parts of the garden, where bamboos and ferns abound. There are magnificent specimens of davidia hanging out their handkerchief-like bracts in June. The climbing hydrangea ascends a tree trunk as it would in its native Japanese forests, and throughout evidence that man's hand has interfered is minimal. This is a garden at its peak of beauty in May and early June.

Opposite. Mixed planting of shrubs and herbaceous plants skilfully grown in the cottage-garden style at East Lambrook Manor

Above left. Cherries in bloom beside the old stone bridge in the woodland and bog garden at Minterne

Above right. One of the recessed pools at Hestercombe, fed with water from a carved stone mask

Hestercombe

Cheddon Fitzpaine, Somerset. Two-and-a-half miles north of Taunton off the A361. Headquarters of the Somersetshire Fire Brigade. Permission to visit the garden can be obtained from the Chief Fire Officer, weekends preferred.

The great terraced garden of Hestercombe probably represents the peak of the collaboration between Sir Edwin Lutyens as architect and Miss Gertrude Jekyll as gardener, and despite the fact that it has long ceased to be in private ownership and has not been acquired by the National Trust or any other garden-minded body, it is remarkably well preserved. Various buildings and erections required by the fire service obtrude a little on the house, and the woodlands and valley are overgrown, but the terraces, with their elaborate parterre, their narrow canal pools for irises, their constant change of level, with curving flights of stairs repeating the line of curving walls and shell-like alcoves, remain as Lutyens designed them.

Some of the rich planting of perennials with which Miss Jekyll habitually softened the sharp architectural outlines of such gardens as this is also still here, and the stone-pillared pergola is heavy with clematis, vines and other climbers. Herbaceous perennials occupy many of the borders, but the big triangular beds which fill in the X-pattern of the parterre are now planted in summer mainly with dahlias, which might not have been to Miss Jekyll's liking, though they are undeniably effective.

The mellow stone orangery still stands apart in a cool, simpler setting of its own, with open lawn and a few trees; and, of course, there is the famous view for miles to south and west across the Vale of Taunton Deane.

Stourhead

near Mere, Wiltshire. Three miles north-west of Mere off the B3092 from Mere to Frome. The National Trust. Open daily throughout the year.

Perhaps the most beautiful and best-preserved example, remaining in Britain, of the 18th-century landscape style. Stourhead was designed by an amateur, Henry Hoare, who started work about 1740 by damming a steep-sided valley and so creating a large lake, around which he proceeded to build a domed Pantheon, a Temple of Flora and a Temple of the Sun, all in classical style, as well as some more rustic constructions including a very large and elaborate grotto and a cottage. A fine stone bridge with five arches crosses one end of the lake, a 14th-century market cross of considerable beauty and brought from Bristol, stands near the entrance to the garden and even the church has been brought into this elysian picture. The whole is encircled by a broad path which leads around the lake, past the various architectural

objects, with continually changing views across the water and up the thickly-wooded sides of the valley.

The planting has been considered with as much care in picture making as the placing of the various buildings and ornaments, but has inevitably changed with the passing years. In the present century many exotic trees and shrubs, which were not available when Henry Hoare first made the garden, have been added or used as replacements for those that had died or were on the decline, and these include some of the best rhododendrons, magnolias, and conifers.

This is a garden that is beautiful throughout the year, but which has peak seasons of colour in late spring and early summer and again in autumn. There are those who contend, however, that too much colour is a distraction in a landscape so well composed as this, and that Stourhead is most delightful when there are few plants in bloom.

50

Wilton House

Wilton, Wiltshire. Two-and-a-half miles west of Salisbury on the A30 to Shaftesbury. Privately owned. Open Tuesday to Saturday and on Bank Holidays from April to September, also on Sundays in August and the first three Sundays in September.

Garden making on the grand scale continued at Wilton House for a period of about 200 years, starting with the Earl of Pembroke about 1632 and finishing with the 11th Earl in the late 18th and early 19th centuries. It all began with a garden in the Italian Renaissance style designed by Isaac de Caus. This was later extended by the 8th earl, around 1700, in the formal landscape manner which was then just beginning to become fashionable. The tiny River Nadder, little more than a brook, was dammed, and a few years later the 9th earl, assisted by the architect Roger Morris, designed a Palladian bridge to span it. This was the first bridge of its type to be built as a garden feature, and it was soon copied elsewhere, by William Kent at Stowe (see p. 76), and also at Prior Park, Bath (see p. 86). By this time, little trace of the original garden by Isaac de Caus can have remained except for a number of cedar trees, some of which are still growing and have attained an enormous size.

Throughout the 18th century the transformation of the garden to the landscape style continued, with parkland sweeping right to the walls of the mansion itself. William Chambers, who designed the pagoda and many of the temples at Kew, worked also at Wilton during this period; but the greatest expansion, to include about 100 acres of land, occurred under the 11th earl between 1794 and 1827. Though much of this work was the completion of the landscape schemes initiated by his predecessors, he also created a formal Italian garden near the house, and built an Italian-style loggia to overlook it, thus restoring something of the formal setting as it may originally have been over 300 years ago.

Above, the 18th-century Palladian bridge at Wilton House, across the dammed River Nadder, and below, the early 19th-century formal garden

The South-West

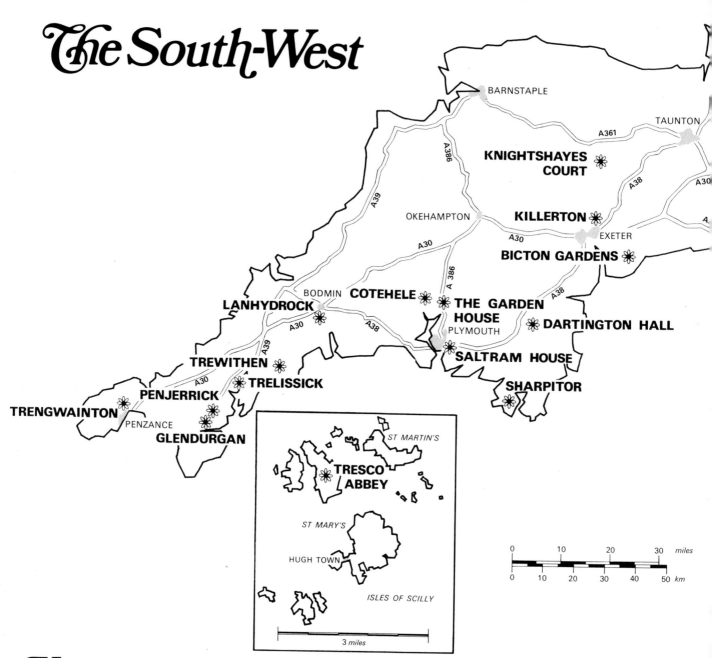

Here, in the leg-like peninsular that stretches out towards the Atlantic and contains the counties of Devon and Cornwall, the gardener begins to feel the full benefits of a milder climate provided by the warm sea of the Gulf Stream Drift lapping the shores to north and south. This is the great area of sub-tropical woodland gardens, where tree ferns grow luxuriantly and camellias are in flower before Christmas. They are gardens that have grown up and expanded as the influx of plants from Asia, America and Australasia has increased in volume as the result of 19th and 20th-century explorations. Many of them are gardens which long since burst any formal bounds they may once have had, flowing out into the surrounding woodlands and valleys wherever room could be found to plant a few more acquisitions, the flowers of which might not be seen for another generation. Tree magnolias and tree rhododendrons abound. Camellias grow as freely as laurels elsewhere. Genistas from the warm

Canary Islands survive and fill the air with fragrance, and a great many other rare and beautiful trees and shrubs are grown as they can be grown in few other parts of the British Isles.

The most esoteric of all these gardens, one that really does seem to transport the visitor to a different continent, is at Tresco Abbey in the Isles of Scilly, thirty-five miles from Penzance at the south-western tip of Cornwall, from which the islands can be reached by sea or air.

So specialised has this south-west gardening become that it has attracted a literature of its own. *Shrubs for the Milder Counties* by the late Arnold Foster, who himself created a remarkable hillside garden, Eagle's Nest, above Zennor in Cornwall, is the classic example of this kind, but it is now unhappily out of print.

Rhododendrons at The Garden House in Devon

Bicton Gardens

Colaton Raleigh, Devon. One mile south of Colaton Raleigh on the A376 from Newton Poppleford to Exmouth. Privately owned. Open daily from April to the end of September.

These wonderful gardens are divorced from the house which is now separately administered as an agricultural college, but this matters not at all since they were never designed either as a setting for this house or as a viewpoint from it. Instead, situated some distance away in a wide and shallow valley, they centre upon a classical temple and orangery, with the church as a second focus of interest and the notably fine palm house as a third.

The gardens themselves fall into several quite distinct sections, some linked and enhancing each other by their contrast in styles, others quite separate and to be enjoyed in isolation. In the first category comes the formal garden; walled on each side and backed by the temple and orangery, it looks across the valley to the arboretum and woodlands beyond. A deep, stone-balustraded terrace separates the upper terrace from the water garden below and provides an almost aerial view of it. This section consists of a large rectangular pool surrounded on three sides by a canal. There is a fine central fountain and a number of delightful bronze statues on pedestals. A wide avenue cut through the trees permits an uninterrupted view of the far hilltop which is surmounted by a large stone obelisk. There are ancient cedars on the upper terrace, large beds and vases filled with flowers in season, and the walls are clothed with the evergreen leaves and large white flowers of the spectacular and exceedingly lovely shrub, *Magnolia grandiflora*.

The woodlands extend for a considerable distance and are terminated by a hermitage and rock garden, the latter a recent addition. Much older is an extraordinary conglomeration of rocks in front of a circular garden house or pavilion, built of stone, and now used to house a notable collection of shells. Yet another section of this remarkable garden is devoted largely to American trees and shrubs arranged in island beds separated by paths and glades of grass. One of the greenhouses is used for an interesting display of plants of economic importance and there are several others, each devoted to a particular type of plant and providing an ideal opportunity to see them grouped in this way.

The pool, canals and balustraded terraces in Bicton Gardens, backed by a temple and orangery, were made in the mid-18th century in the French style

The Garden House

Buckland Monachorum, Devon. Two miles west of Yelverton off the A386. Privately owned. Open every Wednesday from mid-April to mid-September.

The Garden House was once a vicarage, and is pleasantly placed at the edge of a small but steep valley. This had been terraced for cultivation, possibly in mediaeval times, and at the foot of the valley there are the remains of the entrance and staircase tower of a 14th-century house. The present garden, made partly on these terraces, partly on the slope to one side and on the flatter ground above the valley, is recent, work having commenced in 1945. It is of great interest, both because of the very fine collection of plants it contains and because of the skill with which they have been associated to obtain special colour or seasonal effects. One terrace is planted entirely in shades of blue, yellow and white, another in white, pink, rose, crimson and purple, and so on. Rhododendrons, azaleas and camellias thrive on the upper terraces where the soil is acid, but the lower terraces are alkaline from long cultivation, and here shrub roses, philadelphus and other lime-tolerant shrubs are used. There are flowering cherries in the old orchard flanking the drive, and rock plants are grown in raised beds.

Great care has been taken to select only the very best varieties of each kind of tree, shrub and herbaceous perennial planted in this garden, which has been made by a connoisseur of good plants, who is also keenly interested in the problem of using permanent labour-saving plants to obtain the maximum possible effect. The old walls have been covered with climbing plants, including clematis and wisteria; while in the damper soil in the bottom of the valley, paths lead between beds carpeted with crimson mossy saxifrage, golden globe flower (trollius) and similar plants.

The Garden House stands above a series of terraces probably originally created for the cultivation of vines and now adapted for ornamental plants

Cotehele

Calstock, Devon. Four miles south-west of Tavistock off the A390 road to Callington. The National Trust. Open daily, except Mondays, from April to September, but only on Wednesdays, Saturdays, Sundays and Bank Holiday Mondays from October to March.

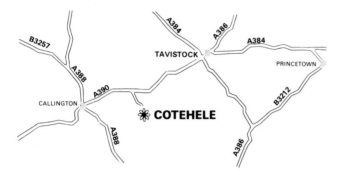

The house, situated high over the Tamar valley, is one of the most notable examples of late mediaeval architecture in the country and, because of its fame, rather overshadows the garden which is, nevertheless, delightful and well worth a visit in its own right. There are, in fact, four more or less separate gardens, one a series of terraces retained by low stone walls in front of the house; another a woodland glen; a third a meadow garden with ornamental trees planted in rough grass in which daffodils and bluebells are naturalised, and the fourth a formal garden with circular pool, lawns, herbaceous borders backed by yew hedges and a bronze statue. But artistically it is the first two that are by far the most important, one leading to and complementing the other.

The view down the lovely woodland glen at Cotehele with the River Tamar and viaduct in the valley below. The domed stone dovecot is very old

The terraces are almost severe in their simplicity, planted with climbing roses and flowers in season and with a fine old magnolia permitting only a veiled view of the glen below. This falls steeply to the Tamar, framing in its heavily-wooded slopes a lovely view of the river and a distant stone viaduct that crosses it. In the foreground is an old stone dovecot with domed roof and a thatched summer-house. A stream flows through the glen feeding several pools and cascades on its way, and the whole glen is densely planted with trees, shrubs, bamboos, palms, herbaceous plants and ferns. There are rhododendrons, azaleas, hydrangeas and eucryphias in plenty, but no type of plant predominates and the intention has been to create an effect of almost tropical luxuriance rather than to make a collection of rare exotic plants. It is a delightful piece of landscaping in which full use has been made of the natural beauty of the site and of the luxuriant growth possible in the damp and mild climate.

Knightshayes Court

Bolham, Tiverton, Devon. One-and-a-half miles north of Tiverton on the A396 to Bampton. Privately owned. Open on Thursdays in April, May and June.

The gardens have been made over a long period and most successfully combine formal features dating from the mid-19th century with 20th-century woodland planting. The house stands on rising ground with parkland to the south, a dell and pool to the west and woodland to the north and east. Ample terraces give a suitable appearance of stability to the house, link it with the woodland and provide some of the finest views of the park and surrounding country. On these terraces there are several gardens enclosed by high hedges of yew on some of which running hounds have been cut. There is a pleasant variation in the treatment of these gardens, one being quite heavily but permanently planted, another almost devoid of plants and with a circular pool in the centre. Below the terrace walls a flat scree bed provides suitable conditions for a good collection of alpine plants.

In the woodland equal care has been taken to provide the correct growing conditions for each type of plant. There are peat beds for those that like acid soil, shady places for those that dislike sunshine, and more open planning for the plants that enjoy their sunlight filtered through leaves. Small herbaceous plants, bulbs and ground cover are given as much care and attention as the more spectacular trees and shrubs, which include a great many rhododendrons, camellias and magnolias. In all, this is a garden combining in full measure all the qualities of good gardening, design, rich and varied plant material together with first-rate maintenance and attention to detail.

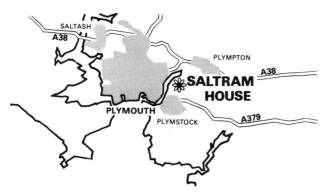

Left. A scree bed for choice alpine plants beneath the terrace gardens at Knightshayes Court

Above right. Bluebell time at Saltram House, and (below) lead sphinxes by the wood-built orangery

Saltram House

Plymouth, Devon. Three-and-a-half miles east of Plymouth off the A38 to Plympton. The National Trust. Open daily, except Tuesdays, from April to September.

The large, rather severely styled, white mansion stands on a little ridge which slopes gently to the south to give good views of the Cattewater and Plymouth Sound, and to the north-west falls much more steeply to the River Plym, which widens into an estuary at this point. It is surrounded by nearly 300 acres of land, much of which has been landscaped in the late 18th-century manner with clumps and belts of trees interspersed with grazing; but the garden proper is on the summit of the ridge, thrust out from the house like a long finger pointing westwards. It consists largely of lawn surrounded by trees and broken by more trees and large groups of shrubs which include many exotic kinds such as rhododendrons, azaleas, magnolias and camellias.

Near the house are the ruins of an old chapel partly hidden by an enormous blue Atlas cedar, and further away, placed back against the trees where it is concealed from the house and suddenly comes into view as one walks across the lawn, is an unusual orangery, largely constructed of wood and with two lead sphinxes guarding its door. Other buildings of interest in the garden are an octagonal pavilion at the extreme west tip and a small classical temple on the steep slope to the north, now completely enclosed in woodland, but no doubt originally intended to command fine views of the Plym.

An oval, gravelled area between the ruined chapel and the orangery is ringed by large shrubs, including a magnificent eucryphia, to form a sheltered area in which to display in summer the orange trees in their elegant white, boat-shaped tubs, and blue African lilies (agapanthus) in tubs of more normal shape.

Lanhydrock

Bodmin, Cornwall. Two-and-a-half miles south-east of Bodmin on the B3268 to Lostwithiel. The National Trust. Open on Wednesdays and Saturdays from April to September.

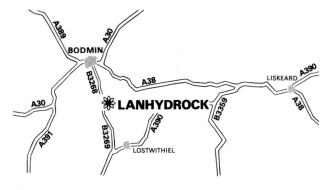

Man and nature have combined to make Lanhydrock a place of exceptional beauty. The grey stone Jacobean house stands on the east side of the heavily-wooded valley of the River Fowey. It is approached by a long drive flanked by a great avenue of sycamores, now past maturity and gradually being replaced by beech which also covers much of the surrounding hills. The house itself and its neighbouring church stand close against one such hill which forms a backdrop to them and provides some of the finest views over the house, gardens and park.

It was not until the mid-19th century that the formal terraces were made in front of and to one side of the house, but so cleverly have they been contrived, with low castellated walls to separate one from the other and to link all with the lovely two-storey gatehouse which stands at the head of the avenue, that they might have been there for 300 years. Even the handsome bronze urns which decorate them are in period.

brought from France where they were made by Louis Ballin, goldsmith to Louis XIV. The terraces are planted with clipped yews, bedding plants and roses, while the woodlands contain many rhododendrons, azaleas and other exotic shrubs.

The north face of the hill, immediately behind the house, has been treated in a more open park-like manner with gravelled paths winding gently upwards between good trees and shrubs grown, for the most part, as individual specimens. To the south-east the land falls more steeply and here a further great area of woodland has been planted about a century ago.

The gardens at Lanhydrock combine formal, landscape and woodland features. Above is one of the bronze urns, similar to those at Versailles, which ornament the parterres around the house, seen below. The two-storey gatehouse was built in the mid-17th century

Glendurgan

Mawnan Smith, Cornwall. One mile south-west of Mawnan Smith and four miles south-west of Falmouth on the road to Helford Passage. The National Trust. Open on Mondays and Wednesdays from April to September, also on Fridays in April and May.

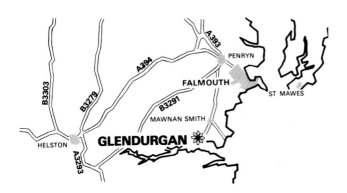

The house stands at the head of a long and steep-sided valley, which runs southwards and then curls away to the west to emerge on the estuary of the Helford River and the little hamlet of Durgan. This very interesting site, with its unusual variety of contours, has been used to create a landscape, part parkland, part wood, and contains one unexpected but effective formal feature – a great maze planted in laurel and placed on the slope where the valley curves, so that from the far side it can be viewed in plan. Near the house is a rectangular walled garden in which there are good shrubs and many climbing plants.

Apart from these features of design and the considerable natural beauty of the site, Glendurgan is notable for its collection of trees and shrubs, including some of the finest specimens of drimys to be found anywhere in the British Isles. There are many rhododendrons, including some of the more tender kinds for which Cornish gardens are famous, and it is of note that in the damp grassland below the maze, the Asiatic *Primula helodoxa* has become happily naturalised.

The maze at Glendurgan, formed in laurel and with a central whitebeam, is an unexpectedly formal feature in what is mainly a wild garden. The well-planted valley runs down to the Helford River

Dartington Hall

Dartington, Devon. Two miles north-east of Totnes off the A384 to Buckfastleigh. Privately owned. Open daily throughout the year.

Some parts of Dartington Hall are very old indeed, and the banqueting hall is said to date from the 14th century. So, probably, does the tilting yard which now forms the hub around which the garden has been redesigned. For, though gardening of a kind has been carried on here for centuries and some of the oaks, chestnuts and beeches are certainly very old, there was little organised garden remaining when Dartington Hall was purchased by Mr and Mrs Elmhirst in 1925. They sought the advice of numerous experts, including Mr Avray Tipping and Mr Stewart Lynch. However, in the period to 1939, design was largely in the hands of the American landscape architect, Mrs Beatrix Farrand, and from 1946 the work was continued by the British designer, Mr Percy Cane. The result is one of the finest gardens of this century in which the fullest use has been made of the natural features of the site and of the adjacent countryside.

The hall and its accompanying buildings stand on high ground with a wide and deep valley to one side, beyond which the encircling hillside ends abruptly in a promontory from which the finest views of the countryside, and even, on a clear day, of the distant sea, are to be obtained. It was in this valley that there was once a tiltyard, and its sides had been scooped out in great steps to serve as terraces for spectators. All this has been turned to good account as an open-air theatre was required and this was, of course, the ideal site. The flat floor of the valley and the terraces have all been covered with well-mown turf, and stone steps sweep down into it from the upper end and out of it to the lower part of the valley, so creating a fine vista right through it and out into the park-like scenery beyond. To one side are twelve large, close-trimmed Irish yews which heighten the dramatic tension.

From the house side the valley is overlooked by a path backed by a flower border and clematis-covered wall. This leads to the woodland garden which fills the upper part of the valley and is well planted with azaleas, rhododendrons, camellias, magnolias and hydrangeas, the whole treatment being natural in style, in contrast to the formality of the tiltyard.

The ridge on the far side gets yet a third treatment; first an open meadow with a fine view back to the house, and then a long-grassed glade closed on both sides by trees but open at the end where a circular stone bastion has been built to command the finest views of the country, the tiltyard and the old buildings beyond. Near this point, too, Henry Moore has placed the stone statue of a Reclining Woman which he carved specially for Dartington Hall. It is one of several pieces of interesting sculpture which enrich the garden. From this high ridge a considerable flight of stone steps leads down between banks of heather to the lower lawn below the tiltyard and so back up the hill to the mansion with its own pleasant and spacious courtyard garden.

Sharpitor

Salcombe, Devon. One-and-a-half miles south-west of Salcombe on the lane to Bolt Head. The National Trust. Open daily throughout the year.

The charm of this little-known garden lies partly in its situation, high above Salcombe Harbour with magnificent views both of it and of the coast to Prawle Point, and partly in the rich collection of plants with which it was stocked between 1912 and 1937 by the late Mr Otto Overbeck. Of design there is very little, though at house level the ground has been terraced and there are twin herbaceous borders with an attractive life-size bronze statue of a young girl between them. But for the most part this is a plantsman's garden, with paths winding up and down the steep hillside to give access to the beds packed with good trees, shrubs and herbaceous plants, many of them too tender to thrive in any but the warmest of British gardens.

Trewithen

Grampound, Cornwall. Two miles west of Grampound on the A390 from St Austell to Probus. Privately owned. Open on Tuesdays and Thursdays from March to June and during September.

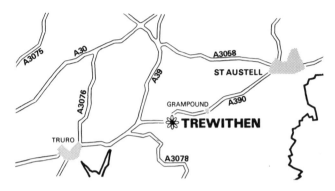

This garden was made to contain an almost unrivalled collection of rhododendrons, camellias, magnolias and other exotic trees and shrubs but with an uncommonly firm sense of design which adds greatly to the attraction of the plants.

However, the site itself offers no great help in this, being more or less level, but the house is a beautiful example of 18th-century architecture. It has been permitted to dominate the main garden which extends as a long wedge of lawn based upon its south front and hemmed in by trees and shrubs. This diminishing perspective has the effect of exaggerating the apparent size of the garden and, in particular, of giving a great sense of depth. Beyond this lawn a path cuts through the woodland at right angles and is flanked by a ditch in which countless moisture-loving plants thrive, beside which are hundreds of evergreen azaleas and camellias. At one point there is a large hollow, said to have been used in times past as a cockpit and now containing some of the most luxuriant planting, including a tree fern centrally placed so that its great fan of fronds catches the eye like a huge and elaborately decorated shield.

A further feature, to the west of the main vista, is a large woodland garden in which some of the finest individual rhododendrons and magnolias grow. Near the house a walled garden provides yet another change in style as well as shelter and support for a great many climbing plants which provide many good ideas for wall planting.

Opposite. The upper picture is of the open-air theatre at Dartington Hall and below it is the great stairway leading to the upper woodland glades

Above right. Sharpitor garden and the magnificent view to the Salcombe estuary

Right. Rhododendrons and camellias at Trewithen

Tresco Abbey

Tresco, Isles of Scilly. Reached by boat from Hugh Town, St Mary. Privately owned. Open daily, except Sundays, throughout the year.

The garden of Tresco Abbey has been called a paradise garden as plants from so many parts of the world thrive in it. This is possible because of the mild climate of the Isles of Scilly and of the shelter of a great belt of evergreen trees to the west and north which protect it from Atlantic gales.

Tresco Abbey stands on a rocky eminence with the garden lying around and below it. Full use has been made of the great natural outcrops of stone to construct banks separated by wide walks. In the lower parts a more formal plan has been followed, but everywhere design tends to be obscured by the luxuriant growth of plants. The general impression is of a sub-tropical garden with palms, tree ferns, giant agaves, aloes, fragrant genistas and pelargoniums permanently estab-

lished and often grown to great size. There are succulents in vast numbers and mesembryanthemums with brilliantly coloured flowers that grow, not only in the garden itself, but also in many other parts of the island as garden escapes or planted by cottagers. This is true also of other plants, including the blue African lily (agapanthus) and New Zealand flax with its huge sword-shaped leaves which will be found naturalised in the sand dunes to the south.

Australasian plants thrive particularly well at Tresco Abbey and so do many plants from South Africa. Giant echiums from the Canaries, with tall spikes of blue flowers, are another of the spectacular features which arrest even those visitors with little horticultural knowledge. An entirely non-horticultural feature is the covered courtyard, known as Valhalla, in which ships' figureheads are displayed.

The gardens at Tresco Abbey were started in the mid-19th century by Mr Augustus Smith and have been continually in the care of his descendants ever since, the collection of plants being enlarged and diversified all the time.

Killerton

Broad Clyst, Devon. Seven miles north-east of Exeter off the A38 from Exeter to Cullompton. The National Trust. Open daily throughout the year.

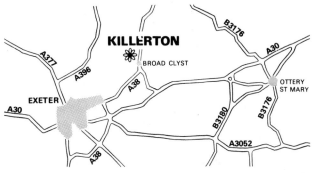

Here, in one of the great privately owned arboreta of the 19th century, planting has continued to the present day. The 15-acre site on the south slope of Killerton Clump is a particularly happy one, both because it is so sheltered and has such good air drainage that many trees and shrubs, normally regarded as rather tender, thrive and also because it commands splendid views towards Exeter and of Dartmoor to the south-west. The property belonged to the Aclands for more than 200 years, but extensive planting of tree and shrubs did not begin until the 1820s when Sir Thomas Acland began work with the help of the Exeter nurseryman Robert Veitch.

The plan, as of most arboreta, is simple, consisting in the main of paths zig-zagging up the steep hillside, but the planting has been carried out cleverly, with plenty of variation between broad-leaved and coniferous trees and a sufficient underplanting of flowering shrubs to provide colour over a long season. One of the paths, known as the Beech Walk because of the fine old beeches which line it, is sufficiently wide and long to provide a good vista through the wood and sufficient openings have been left to permit views of the countryside as one ascends the hill. An excellent guide book is available describing the most notable specimens that will be seen, but even those with no particular interest in rare trees and shrubs will find this a delightful garden on account of its natural beauty.

At the foot of the hill, where the ground levels out, the planting is more open, with some fine Japanese cherries and beds of rhododendrons and evergreen azaleas set in wide lawns. There is also an attractive terrace garden adjoining the house, laid out in rectangular beds and planted with herbaceous perennials and dwarf shrubs. At one end of the lawn is an interesting Victorian rustic summer-house and a short distance away across the fields, near the chapel, are two of the largest tulip trees (*Liriodendron tulipifera*) in the country.

Opposite. An aerial view of Tresco Abbey and its gardens sheltered by evergreen trees from Atlantic gales

Top. The hillside woodland at Killerton seen from the terrace near the house which has been permanently planted as a parterre with dwarf shrubs and many herbaceous perennials

Bottom. The long stone stairway at Tresco Abbey which leads from the bottom garden to the statue of Neptune of the upper terrace. It is flanked with palms, cordylines and many other sub-tropical plants

Penjerrick

Budock, Cornwall. Two miles south-west of Falmouth on the road to Mawnan Smith. Privately owned. Open on Sundays and Wednesdays throughout the year.

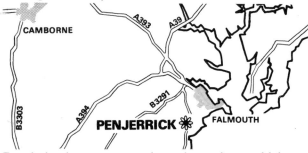

Rhododendron growers throughout the world know the name Penjerrick, because it has been given to one of the most beautiful hybrid varieties which originated here in the early years of the century. The original plants may still be seen growing together with Cornish Cross, another of the great rhododendrons raised at Penjerrick.

The garden occupies a shallow but sheltered valley and at one point a road cuts across it, but this is sunk in so deep a cutting that, like a ha-ha, one is unaware of its presence until one reaches it. A wooden bridge gives access to the lower garden which contains a small lake, a great many tree ferns and gunneras and what must be one of the largest weeping beech trees in the country. However, it is in the upper garden between the road and the long low house that the main glory of Penjerrick lies. In April, May and early June

there are few gardens which contain such a splendour of colour and richness of fragrance in so comparatively small a space. The climate is sufficiently mild for many of the more tender rhododendrons to thrive and these, together with hardier kinds, embothriums, pieris, tree ferns and many other fine trees and shrubs have been planted with a lavish generosity. Design is simple but adequate, a long lawn descending the slope to the south from the house and providing a more·or less uninterrupted view over both gardens. This view is channelled by the trees and shrubs which on the eastern side extend to a considerable depth and are penetrated by winding paths to reveal ever-changing delights and unusual plants.

Trelissick

King Harry Ferry, Cornwall. Three miles south of Truro on the B3289 off the A39 from Truro to Falmouth. The National Trust. Open on Wednesdays, Thursdays, Fridays and Bank Holiday Mondays from March to September.

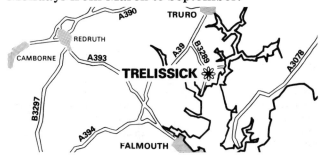

This large woodland garden occupies a site of great natural beauty at the head of Carrick Roads, where the open Falmouth estuary splits up into a more complex system of channels and backwaters. The site is undulating, but almost all of it is at a fairly high level, looking down on the river and estuary and commanding numerous fine views, some of Falmouth to the south, some of Tregothnan to the north. Suitable vantage points have been prepared from which these views can be enjoyed, but the design of the garden as a whole is inward rather than outward looking and even the house plays no significant part in it. This is, in fact, a very typical example of many such gardens made during the late 19th and early 20th centuries for the cultivation and display of the great variety of hardy and near-hardy trees and shrubs which were then pouring into the country from all parts of the world.

Trelissick is specially famed for its rhododendrons and camellias but it also contains a great many other fine plants, and under the care of the National Trust is being further enriched with a particularly comprehensive collection of hydrangeas to provide colour and interest in summer and early autumn. The planning is pleasantly varied, open and meadow-like in some places, well wooded in others with paths winding through the tall trees and emerging here and there into shrub-ringed glades.

Trengwainton

Penzance, Cornwall. Two miles west of Penzance off the A3071 to St Just. The National Trust. Open on Wednesdays, Fridays, Saturdays and Bank Holiday Mondays from March to September.

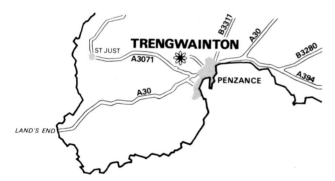

In design this is a curious garden since, in the main, it lies beside a very long drive leading from the road to the house. A stream runs parallel with the drive and beyond it is a belt of woodland, the one providing scope for the planting of many candelabra primulas and other moisture-loving plants, and for the creation of a series of pleasant cascades, the latter giving suitable overhead cover for rhododendrons, azaleas, hydrangeas, pieris and many other shrubs.

Near the entrance is a series of rectangular gardens surrounded by high brick walls which provide protection for the more tender plants and support for climbers. These are treated as a series of botanical gardens, a collector's paradise in which it is the beauty or rarity of each individual specimen, rather than any overall effect, which matters. Even the gravelled turn-around for cars in front of the house is encircled by splendid rhododendrons, and the lawns which flank the house on two sides are hemmed in by more of these magnificent shrubs. Beside one of these is a rocky mound, and it, too, has its covering of dwarf rhododendrons, mainly the small-leaved blue and purple-flowered varieties.

Opposite. Rhododendrons at Penjerrick, near Falmouth

Above. In the woodland garden at Trelissick

Below. The flower-lined stream at Trengwainton

65

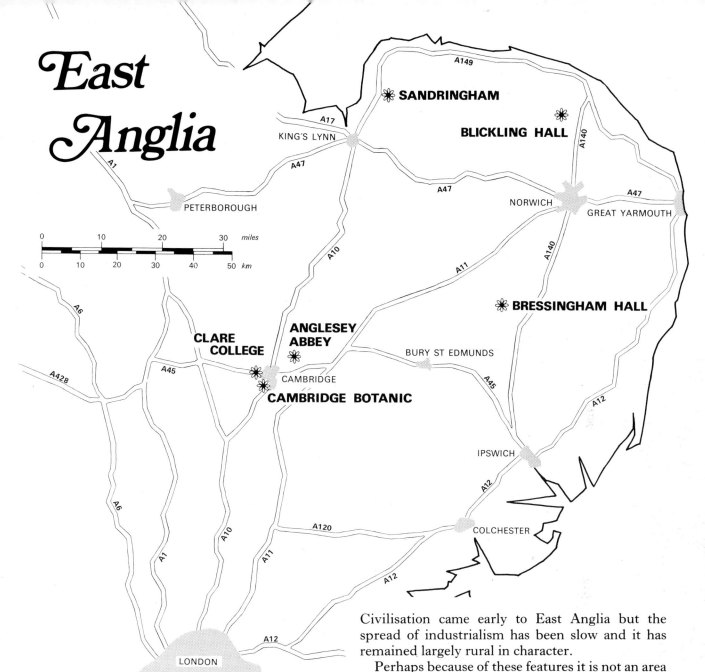

East Anglia

The climate of East Anglia is dry, especially to the south, in Essex, where a considerable seed-growing industry has grown up because of the good prospects of ripening the crop. It is an area without any considerable hills, and the whole area of the Fenland, extending southwards from The Wash for 50 miles, is notably flat. But much of East Anglia is undulating and well wooded, with a restful but very pleasing scenic character. Though the soil of the Fenland is sandy or peaty, qualities which have attracted the greatest concentration of commercial bulb growing in the British Isles, a great band of chalk runs right through East Anglia from Cambridge in the south-west to Cromer in the north-east, and from this belt southwards to the Thames the soil is mainly rich and heavy, overlying clay.

Civilisation came early to East Anglia but the spread of industrialism has been slow and it has remained largely rural in character.

Perhaps because of these features it is not an area where great gardens abound, though there are now some notable exceptions. Away to the north-east the magnificent Tudor mansion, Blickling Hall, has stimulated gardeners of various generations to give it a suitably beautiful setting. To the north-west, not far from The Wash, is Sandringham, a favourite country residence of the Royal family, the gardens of which have engaged the attention of many well-known designers. But one of the most remarkable of all East Anglian gardens, which perhaps owes most to the topography of the land, is that made in the present century by the late Lord Fairhaven at Anglesey Abbey on the southern edge of the Fenland. Here, stimulated in part by a passion for the culture of the 17th century, in part by the vast horizons of this flat land, he created a series of tree avenues which carry the eye outwards, and a series of enclosures which give protection from the wind, enriching both with a collection of statuary and ornament unrivalled in a 20th-century British garden.

The redesigned parterre at Blickling Hall

Anglesey Abbey

Stow-cum-Quy, Cambridgeshire. Six miles northeast of Cambridge on the B1102 to Fordham from the A45. The National Trust. Open on Wednesdays, Thursdays, Saturdays, Sundays and Bank Holiday Mondays from Easter to October.

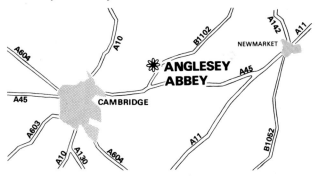

Despite its name Anglesey Abbey has not been in ecclesiastical use since the dissolution of the monasteries in the 16th century, and the present house, built about 1600, has always been a private residence. Until it was purchased in 1926 by the late Lord Fairhaven and his brother, the garden consisted of little more than parkland with some fine trees. The great tree avenues, the yew-enclosed rose garden, the unusual semi-circular herbaceous garden, the newly-planted pinetum as well as the many fine statues, urns and architectural structures which make this garden so unique to-day, have all been added since that date. Lord Fairhaven was a student of 17th- and 18th-century art and culture, and in planning and planting his great garden – it covers well over 100 acres – he was strongly influenced by the ideas then current. He planted avenues which are wide and open ended, leading the eye on to the surrounding country, and he also planted avenues that are narrow and enclosed and serve primarily as a

background for statuary or as a contrast to the more open spaces. In the use and placing of ornament he showed considerable ingenuity and variety. One splendid urn stands by a deep pool, once a quarry, which captures its reflection. A temple in the Chinese style, with a magnificent porphyry vase, is almost hidden among the evergreen trees; whereas another temple, formed of pillars in the classical style and surrounding a marble copy of Bernini's David, stands in a circle of yew in the middle of a large glade. In his later years Lord Fairhaven was adding many exotic trees planted for their individual beauty, so that there is at Anglesey Abbey to-day something to interest both the plantsman and those primarily interested in design.

One of the curving borders in the unusually designed herbaceous garden at Anglesey Abbey, near Cambridge

Opposite top. The large rock garden in the Cambridge Botanic Garden is highly decorative and is constructed to reproduce conditions in natural limestone areas

Opposite bottom. The garden at Bressingham Hall with island herbaceous beds and poolside planting

Bressingham Hall

Bressingham, Norfolk. Two-and-a-half miles west of Diss on the A1066 to Thetford. Privately owned. Open on Sundays and Thursdays from the end of May to the beginning of October.

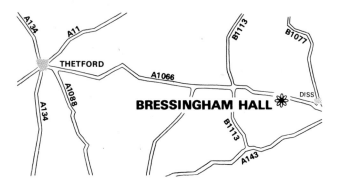

Mr Alan Bloom, who made this garden, is one of the largest commercial growers of hardy herbaceous perennials and rock plants in the country. He also has highly individual ideas on how they should be used to the best effect and to demonstrate these he has laid out several acres around his own house as a display garden. The site is pleasantly enclosed by old trees and is slightly undulating, a character which he has emphasised by a certain amount of soil shifting. He believes that the traditional herbaceous border is neither the best nor the most convenient place in which to grow hardy plants, and that they look better and are more easily cared for in island beds that can be approached from every side. He has, therefore, filled his garden with such beds, of various sizes and shapes, but always with curving edges and set in mown grass which provides comfortable and pleasant paths and open spaces between the beds. In the lowest place there is a pool and a bog garden all worked naturally into the same informal scheme.

All these beds are well planted with an unusually wide selection of hardy plants, since Mr Bloom is keenly interested in plants for their own sake as well as for display. The result is an unusual garden of exceptional beauty and interest.

Cambridge Botanic

Cambridge, Cambridgeshire. On the Trumpington Road, with an entrance also in Bateman Street. University of Cambridge. Open daily, except Sundays and Christmas Day, throughout the year.

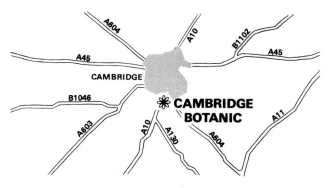

As with most botanical gardens, that at Cambridge is not designed primarily for ornament, though it contains numerous ornamental features. There is a large lake almost divided into two by a narrow ridge that juts out into it and permits the aquatic and bog plants to be viewed from above. There is also a very large limestone rock garden so constructed that it reproduces, as nearly as possible, conditions in various natural limestone areas including the Burren in Ireland, a district noted for its exceptionally rich and varied flora.

But perhaps the most original feature at Cambridge is the way in which the systematic beds, devoted to examples of plants grouped together botanically, have been disposed. Instead of the usual rows of plain rectangular beds, there are a number of island beds with curving edges and of varying size and shape. These are interspaced with mown grass and all are grouped in and around a large oval of clipped hawthorn with radiating arms which separate the great natural groupings as classified in the 19th century by the distinguished English botanists Bentham and Hooker. It is a scheme at once decorative and instructive and it is accompanied by a large display plan which indicates the system of arrangement thus enabling any visitor to identify the various groups.

For the rest, the garden is laid out to a park-like plan with many fine trees well spaced as specimens, informal groupings of shrubs and other plants and a few formal beds for bedding plants in season. There is a good selection of well-stocked greenhouses arranged in a comb-like pattern with some surprisingly tender plants growing in the open, but sheltered, borders between the houses.

Clare College

Fellows' Garden, Cambridge, Cambridgeshire. Can be entered across a bridge over the River Cam behind Clare College or from The Backs. University of Cambridge. Open Monday to Friday, but not on Bank Holidays, all the year.

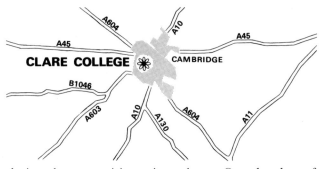

A delightful garden mainly in the Robinsonian style of herbaceous and shrub borders separated by wide areas of grass. There is also a small sunken garden enclosed by a yew hedge and with a formal lily pool, and another small area devoted to fragrant flowers.

It is, however, for the skill of its planting as well as for its lovely views of university buildings, in particular of King's College Chapel, rather than for any special quality in design, that this garden is chiefly memorable. Every plant and shrub has been chosen with the greatest care to play its part in a series of skilfully-designed compositions in colour. One border of shrubs is planned entirely in white; another is designed to obtain the maximum effect from delphiniums; while, near the river, the planning is more open and the softly-coloured stone of the college buildings and of Thomas Grumbold's bridge, built in 1662, provide ample foil for the bright colours of massed bedding plants of many varieties.

Blickling Hall

Blickling, Norfolk. One-and-a-half miles northwest of Aylsham on the B1354 to Saxthorpe. The National Trust. Open on Wednesdays, Thursdays, Saturdays, Sundays and Bank Holiday Mondays from Easter Saturday to the beginning of October.

The gardens at Blickling Hall are of great interest as they were originally laid out over a period of about 150 years, covering both the late Renaissance and landscape periods, and have since been modified to suit modern taste and meet the need to save labour.

The oldest part, the level parterre to the west of the house, probably dates to the early part of the 17th century when the hall itself was built. It may have been a bowling green or a knot garden and until about 1930 was still cut up with elaborate beds filled with flowers in season. Then it was completely redesigned by Mrs Nora Lindsay, the beds being reduced to four large rectangles symmetrically placed and stocked with herbaceous perennials.

Beyond this parterre is a raised balustraded terrace leading to a large woodland garden intersected by a formal pattern of straight rides, and probably made early in the 18th century. The main ride is centred on the parterre and is terminated by a classical temple. Throughout the woodland there are other architectural features, such as an orangery on a raised terrace to the south, a fountain and various statues and urns. Later generations have added many fine exotic trees and shrubs, including rhododendrons and azaleas, which provide much colour in May and June.

To the north-west of the hall is yet a third garden attributed without certainty to Humphrey Repton and probably made towards the end of the 18th century. It is a notable example of its kind with a particularly beautiful crescent-shaped lake, a mile in length, backed by woodland of oak and beech and a massive pyramidal mausoleum.

Opposite. Well-stocked herbaceous borders and the distant spires of King's College Chapel, as seen from one of the small, yew-hedged enclosures in the well-designed Fellows' Garden of Clare College, Cambridge

Below. A vista down one of the woodland avenues at Blickling Hall, seen from the elaborately decorated raised terrace which terminates the main parterre

Right. The water and rock garden at Sandringham. The latter is constructed of exceptionally large blocks of sandstone and is planted on the boldest lines

Sandringham

Norfolk. Eight miles north-east of Kings Lynn off the A149 to Hunstanton. Her Majesty the Queen. Open on Wednesdays and Thursdays from May to September and also on Tuesdays and Fridays in July and August and on Spring and Late Summer Bank Holiday Mondays.

There are two entirely separate gardens at Sandringham, one mainly in the form of a park around the house, and another, known as the Flower Garden, across the road to the east where it adjoins the kitchen garden and is overlooked by the Head Gardener's house.

Most of the park is planted in an open manner with fine trees well displayed as specimens, but in one section to the north, known as the glade, trees and shrubs have been more consciously grouped to form arboreal masses contrasted with level areas of turf. The land falls away to the south-west of the house, allowing for the formation of two lakes, the upper and smaller of which has been most elaborately developed with a rock garden made of massive blocks of red sandstone on its steepest bank. A small, circular stone summer-house built for Queen Mary overlooks it and there is a great deal of surround planting.

A second feature is the long, narrow formal garden at the north end of the house designed by Mr Geoffrey Jellicoe for King George VI. This is contained within double lines of pleached lime trees and is subdivided by box hedges into a number of separate compartments, some heavily planted with a mixture of roses and hardy plants, some plain rectangles of turf. A statue of Father Time completes the vista and a second parallel avenue of limes is terminated by a gilded bronze statue of Kuvera, a Buddhist divinity.

The Flower Garden is well named since it is filled with patterned flower beds in the Victorian manner, is surrounded by high brick walls covered with more flowering plants, and is bisected by a massive flower-covered pergola. It is a great favourite with visitors, especially in summer when it is at its gayest.

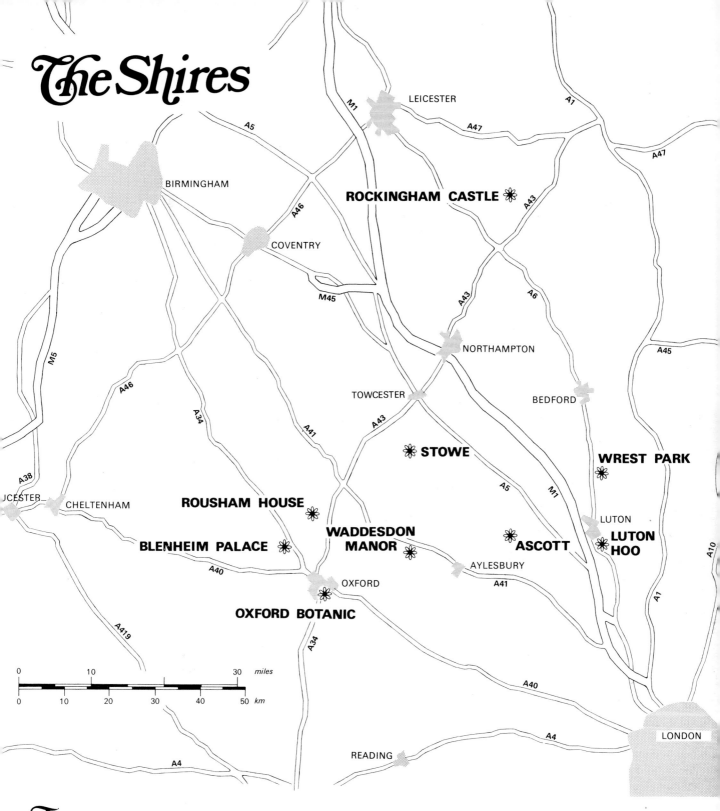

The Shires

BIRMINGHAM

LEICESTER

COVENTRY

ROCKINGHAM CASTLE ✳

NORTHAMPTON

TOWCESTER

BEDFORD

✳ **STOWE**

WREST PARK
✳

CHELTENHAM

ROUSHAM HOUSE
✳

WADDESDON MANOR ✳

✳ **ASCOTT**

LUTON

LUTON HOO
✳

BLENHEIM PALACE ✳

OXFORD

AYLESBURY

OXFORD BOTANIC

JCESTER

LONDON

READING

| 0 | 10 | | 30 | *miles* |
| 0 | 10 | 20 | 30 | 40 | 50 | *km* |

The lattice-work aviary at Waddesdon Manor

This area, sandwiched between East Anglia and the Midlands, contains some of the finest farm land in the country. Its valleys are, for the most part, shallow and its hills low, and they are cut across in every direction by hedgerows and coppices and the lanes required to service the numerous villages and outlying farms. It is country famous for its hunting and it contains a great many fine mansions with gardens or parks to match their importance, some of these properties are also of great antiquity, for example, Rockingham Castle in Northamptonshire.

Because the Shires have always attracted wealth they have also encouraged garden making on the grandest scale. Stowe in Buckinghamshire is 18th-century classical landscape at its most poetic; Wrest Park in Bedfordshire is an outsize example of the French style in England; while at Luton Hoo every kind of style has been combined as a result of Edwardian wealth and exuberance taking over a garden landscaped on the grand scale by Lancelot Brown in the latter half of the 18th century.

Ascott

Wing, Buckinghamshire. Two miles south-west of Leighton Buzzard on the A418 to Aylesbury. The National Trust. Open on Wednesdays, Saturdays and Bank Holiday Mondays from April to September and on some Sundays in July and August.

The house is in the half-timbered neo-Tudor style built, late in the 19th century, on high ground commanding fine views to the Chilterns. The 30-acre garden which completely surrounds it was made at this period and during the early part of the present century by the late Leopold de Rothschild assisted by Sir Harry Veitch, the famous Chelsea nurseryman. It is remarkable for the manner in which numerous formal features have been inserted in what is very largely a park-type garden made to display the individual beauty of an extensive collection of trees. There are many fine cedars – some golden leaved, some blue – mature weeping beeches, swamp cypresses, golden elms, and a great many more, as well as several varieties of variegated holly and fine golden yews.

These trees are, for the most part, widely spaced on lawns so that they can be viewed from any side, and the description 'arboretum' might come to mind were it not for the formal features which give the garden a quite unique character. They include a number of topiary specimens, some conventional peacocks and spirals, but one extraordinary series forming an evergreen sundial, complete with green yew gnomon, box figures and a motto in golden yew stating 'light and shade by turn, but love always'. There are two statuary fountains, one highly elaborate showing a life-size Venus drawn in a shell by sea-horses and attended by cupids and a youth who has caught one of their arrows. These fountains are surrounded by patterned beds planted with gay flowers. There are also rock gardens, one of tufa stone, another very high and providing an almost aerial view of the largest parterre and its delightful planting.

Oxford Botanic

Oxford, Oxfordshire. In the High Street beside the River Cherwell. University of Oxford. Open daily throughout the year, except on Good Friday and Christmas Day.

This comparatively small botanic garden has the distinction of being the oldest in Britain, having been founded by Lord Derby in 1621. The handsome entrance gates, designed by Inigo Jones, bear the date 1632 and the brick walls which surround much of the garden were completed by the following year. Panelled piers surmounted by carved vases were added later, probably about 1700.

The purpose of this garden is academic rather than decorative, yet it has a quiet charm of its own. Beyond the severely functional systematic beds, which fill most of the front portion of the garden, lies a second more ornamental garden with a particularly fine herbaceous border backed by one of the walls, a pleasant rock garden, beds for irises, and other decorative features. There is also a walk beside the river and several greenhouses face this, one containing a good collection of tropical water-lilies.

There are numerous fine trees, including large specimens of sophora, taxodium, manna ash and ginkgo. The lower part of the building which separates the garden from the High Street was originally an orangery and between this and the road is a long, narrow memorial garden, designed after the war by Sylvia Crowe. Though so modern, it follows the old-world tradition of a formal parterre, the beds outlined in box and planted with roses.

Rockingham Castle

Rockingham, Northamptonshire. Three miles north-west of Corby on the A6003 from Kettering to Uppingham. Privately owned. Open on Thursdays and on Bank Holidays (Sundays and Mondays) from Easter to the end of September.

Parts of Rockingham Castle were built by William the Conqueror, and no part of its structure is more recent than Tudor times. It is a lovely and romantic building standing on the edge of a hill commanding splendid views to north, east and west, with Eye Brook reservoir, a notably fine sheet of water, in the middle distance. If there is nothing in its gardens quite to match these architectural and landscape delights they are, nevertheless, very charming with a quality and a history that is entirely their own. There are, in fact, four quite distinct gardens: one, on the west side of the castle, which is at two different levels separated by a yew-lined alley; in the valley below this, a wild garden and bird sanctuary, both comparatively new; to the south a rose garden within a great circle of yew, and beyond this a little park with fine trees well spaced as specimens.

The yew alley is very old, some say 400 years, and Charles Dickens used it as a model for the path between hedges down which the ghost of Lady Deadlock walked in *Bleak House*. The hedge around the rose garden is cut in the same irregular bulging style and looks ancient, though in fact it must be much more recent. But it is entirely in keeping with its surroundings and provides both shelter and background for the roses which grow within it.

The park and the wild garden are both pleasant, well-kept examples of their kind. All available walls have been well planted and even the excavated ruins have been converted into a charming little garden.

Opposite. The bronze fountain of Venus, at Ascott

Top right. The charming systematic beds in the Oxford Botanic Garden. Beyond is Magdalene College Chapel

Right. A garden beside the yew alley at Rockingham

Luton Hoo

Luton, Bedfordshire. Just south of Luton between the A6 and the B653 roads. (Cars enter from the latter only). Privately owned. Open every Wednesday from Good Friday to the end of September.

The park around Luton Hoo was landscaped by Lancelot Brown in the latter half of the 18th century, and the two lakes which he created in the valley to the east of the house, as well as many of the fine belts and clumps of trees which he planted, remain. Further additions were made to the tree planting, especially by the introduction of exotic species in the 19th century, but it was not until the early part of the present century that Luton Hoo was provided with a garden as distinct from a park.

The first addition was the creation of a series of terraces, in the Italian manner, to the south of the house, and then, a decade or so later, a rock garden was added in a small coppice to the east. Since this rock garden is completely encircled by trees, and the terraced gardens are placed to one side away from the main vista, neither obtrudes to any great degree on the Brownian landscape.

The terraces are at three levels: the first plain and flagged; the second larger, rectangular, with grass and surrounding flower borders; the third and lowest far more elaborate, somewhat in the form of a clover leaf with a large circular pool and figure fountain as a central feature, two small domed temples on the flanks and great semi-circular flights of steps leading into it from the middle terrace and down from it to the park. The whole is filled with patterned beds lined with box edging, planted with roses and accented with topiary cones.

The rock garden is in the form of a tree-encircled dell with an informal pool, crossed by a rustic bridge, a cascade and a large grotto. The rock work is well placed but the planting is with herbaceous plants, shrubs, conifers and small trees rather than with true alpine plants.

Stowe

Buckingham, Buckinghamshire. Three miles north-west of Buckingham on the road to Dadford and Silverstone. The Governors of Stowe School. Open occasionally between early April and September.

The finest example of the work of William Kent, the famous 18th-century architect and garden designer, Stowe is in the classical landscape style, and is planned on the largest scale, the great Corinthian arch, erected as a terminal object in the main vista to the south of the building, is three-quarters of a mile distant from it, and the tree-lined avenue continues for two miles to Buckingham itself. Though Kent's name is primarily connected with the design of this garden, many others also played a part in its development. Kent worked on a garden already made by Charles Bridgeman, and the main vista was widened and the Corinthian Arch added after Kent's death.

Because of its size and complexity it is desirable to take a map when visiting the garden for the first time. The splendid view from the south front of the house cannot be missed, nor can the Oxford Bridge, over which the entrance road passes, and the Boycott Pavilions which flank it on both sides. But it would be easy to overlook the Grecian Valley, an almost entirely self-contained feature to the north-east, or the narrow valley, known as the Elysian Fields, which runs parallel to the main vista but is screened by trees. On the far side of the two large lakes, which cross the main vista at right angles, there are more buildings and more vantage points. The Palladian bridge which spans the Octagon Lake at its eastern end is a copy of that at Wilton House, near Salisbury (see p. 51), and the road which crosses it leads up the hill to a curious Gothic Temple. At the south-western extremity of the 11-acre lake is a Temple of Venus with a particularly good view northwards to the Headmaster's house and a classical Rotundo standing on the breast of the hill.

Stowe is now a public school, and its grounds are used for various school activities some of which inevitably

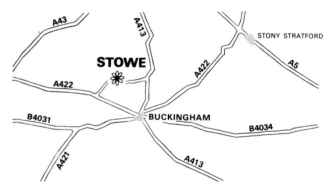

impinge on the classical conception of the garden. There are football fields in the main vista, hard tennis courts by the Palladian bridge and a number of new buildings around the house. Yet the gardens are sufficiently large and firmly designed to survive these additions without much harm, and the school authorities are making every effort to preserve them and where necessary to clear and replant in the appropriate manner.

Opposite. The lowest of the three formal terraces at Luton Hoo was planned early in this century as a rose garden. It is ornamented with two domed temples, one on each side, and a circular stone water basin and fountain. Clipped topiary specimens and surrounding hedge of yew add to the firmness of design

Above. Vanbrugh's elegant Rotundo at Stowe commands views of the Temple of Venus across the lower lake, Queen Caroline's Monument and the Doric Arch Below. The Temple of British Worthies, by William Kent, seen across the lake at the foot of the Elysian Fields, is another of Stowe's remarkable buildings

Rousham House

Steeple Aston, Oxfordshire. Twelve miles north of Oxford off the B4030 from Enstone near Chipping Norton to Bicester. Privately owned. Open on Sundays and Wednesdays during June, July and August.

This is one of the outstanding examples of the landscape style of William Kent, where, as at Stowe (see p. 76), Kent worked on a more formal garden laid out by Charles Bridgeman. It is a much smaller and more intimate garden than Stowe but the same principles have been applied of creating an idealised landscape, seemingly natural but in fact carefully composed to provide a succession of changing views, and with various classical and rustic buildings, statues and ornaments to enhance each picture. Kent intended the circuit to be made in a particular way and provided a special visitors' entrance with a Palladian archway, but this is now closed, and the visitor must approach from the great bowling green on the north side of the house. This is stone balustraded at its far end and has a fine view of the countryside across the River Cherwell and of ruined archways in the middle distance specifically built as an eye-catcher.

The principal landscaping, however, lies to the west in a roughly triangular area enclosed on one side by the river, on another by the road from Steeple Aston, and on the third by an open paddock bounded by a belt of trees. The land slopes to the river and has been planted with clumps and belts of trees to channel and direct the view as the garden is explored. One such viewpoint is a stone-balustraded terrace standing on a seven-arched arcade built in the classical style and known as Praeneste. Another is of a small dell, known as Venus's Vale, containing an octagonal pond and two formal stone cascades as well as a considerable amount of statuary.

There is a straight ride or avenue cut through one of the woods and terminated by an immense statue of Apollo, and another narrower and more winding path which follows a serpentine, stone-channelled rill that flows through a stone basin known as the Cold Bath. One glade has been planted to focus attention on the beautiful 13th-century Heyford Bridge, which carries the main road from Chipping Norton to Bicester, and this glade is backed by a large temple in classical style known as Townsend's Building or the Temple of Echo.

Separate from this landscape garden and older in origin is a walled garden and an immense pigeon house, built in 1685, beside which is a formal rose garden.

Right. Looking across Venus' Vale at Rousham House

Opposite. The water parterre at Blenheim Palace, and (below) Brown's landscape lake and Vanbrugh's bridge

Blenheim Palace

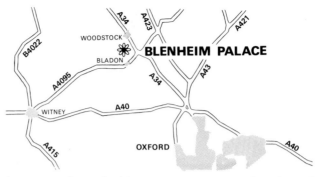

Woodstock, Oxfordshire. Seven miles north-west of Oxford on the A34 to Stratford-upon-Avon. Privately owned. Open daily, except Fridays, from July to mid-September, and on most Mondays, Tuesdays, Wednesdays and Thursdays during the rest of the period from April to October.

Gardening on the grand scale has been carried out three times around Sir John Vanbrugh's palace at Blenheim, built in the reign of Queen Anne as a national gift to the Duke of Marlborough. First came the contemporary gardens of Vanbrugh himself and Henry Wise. These included elaborate parterres and courts close to the house as a fitting setting for its equally elaborate architecture, a canal linking two lakes in the valley to the west, across which Vanbrugh constructed a great stone bridge – so large that it contained 33 rooms in its piers – as a suitably impressive feature in the middle distance of a great vista between trees leading to a Column of Victory.

The parterres were swept away 50 years later by Lancelot Brown who redesigned the grounds as a landscape park, bringing the grass right up to the walls of the mansion. He further dammed the valley thereby joining the two lakes into one, submerging the lower part of Vanbrugh's bridge and thus altering its proportions. In his customary manner he planted clumps and belts of native trees to channel and contain the view and much of this remains to the present day. Finally, in the first quarter of the present century, the 9th Duke of Marlborough employed the French architect, Achille Duchêne, to restore the Great Court in front of the house and to remake formal gardens on both flanks, an elaborate parterre to the north-west and an equally elaborate formal water garden to the south-east, across which one of the finest views of Brown's lake and the surrounding landscape is obtained. These formal gardens restore the Palace to its proper setting. They are on a scale and of an originality that has seldom been equalled in the 20th century and they must rival in their complexity the original parterres of Henry Wise.

Waddesdon Manor

Waddesdon, Buckinghamshire. Five miles north-west of Aylesbury on the A41 to Bicester. The National Trust. Open Wednesday to Sunday inclusive and on Bank Holiday Mondays from late March to late October.

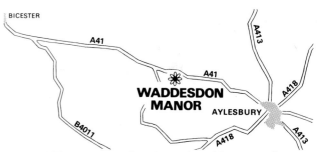

This gloriously uninhibited example of a late Victorian house in the French baroque manner has a garden to match, set in a park which is as British as it could possibly be apart from the overspill of statuary from the formal garden to the south of the house, and the aviary to the north-west. The parkland is full of splendid trees, cedars, wellingtonias, purple, copper and green beeches and many more, often sited as isolated specimens so that their full beauty is displayed. But fine though this park is, it is the formal features at Waddesdon Manor that make the garden a supreme example of its kind. Nowhere else at this period (the formal gardens and aviary were made between 1874 and 1889 by a French designer named Laine) can there have been in England quite such an exuberant use of statuary. The figure fountains are to be compared with those at Cliveden and Hever Castle. The statues of gods and goddesses and many other figures in the classical repertoire not only cluster round the main formal garden but also appear all over the park, either peering at one from shrubberies or from the shelter of fine trees, or their gleaming white forms thrown into high relief by a background of dark evergreens.

The great semi-circular aviary, made of elaborate lattice-work, and its attendant rose-lined garden, has its own animal statuary: vultures, cocks, goats, etc. as well as a big centre-piece of human figures, all rendered yet more flamboyant by the multicoloured macaws which are not confined like so many of the birds, but perch on the outside of the aviary and fly freely from tree to tree.

The elaborate terrace and park at Waddesdon Manor

Wrest Park

Silsoe, Bedfordshire. Nine miles north of Luton on the A6 to Bedford. National Institute of Agricultural Engineering. Open on Saturdays, Sundays and Bank Holidays from April to the end of September.

A great many mansions have had gardens added at a later date. At Wrest Park the opposite has occurred, for though some of the garden was made during the 1830s when the present mansion was being built to replace an earlier one, much of it is far older, some in the semi-formal manner of the early 18th century and some landscaped by Lancelot Brown in the middle of that century.

Where the former mansion stood, a series of terraced parterres was made in the French style to link it with the older gardens. Beyond these is a wide gravelled avenue, flanked with statues, leading to a long formal stretch of water, like a canal, and terminated by a lovely high-domed pavilion designed by Thomas Archer about 1709. The canal is completely enclosed at the sides by woodland, through which radiating avenues are cut in the manner developed by Le Nôtre in his later gardens. Urns, statues or other ornaments stand at intersections of these avenues or occupy glades in the woods, and there are occasional glimpses of the canal and its pavilion.

All this is the Great Garden, created in the first 40 years of the 18th century. To one side, but belonging to the same period, is a bowling green backed by a large pavilion in the Palladian style and said to be the work of Batty Langley. It is interesting because it has two quite different facades, the one facing the bowling green columned and plastered, the other, looking towards the road, brick built and arched.

Lancelot Brown enclosed these gardens in a river-like loop of water, issuing from a rustic bath house and bridge. In Victorian times a second bridge, in Chinese style, was thrown over this water towards its opposite end, and now makes a pleasant feature when seen between the trunks of the large specimen trees scattered about here in a more open park-like manner. The avenue which bisects the parterres is lined with clipped Portugal laurels and passes round a fine marble fountain with lead figures. To one side an orangery, designed in the same style as the house, stands on a low grassed bank, and at a little distance a large group of statuary, representing a hunting party, is partly concealed by a group of blue cedars.

Even the walled nursery, separated from the house by a rose garden and flower borders, has a decorative as well as a utilitarian role, for its entrance gates are elaborately ornamented, bear the date 1836 and carry an inscription stating that the 2nd Earl de Grey enlarged and decorated the garden.

Formal gardens, canal and pavilion at Wrest Park

The Cotswolds

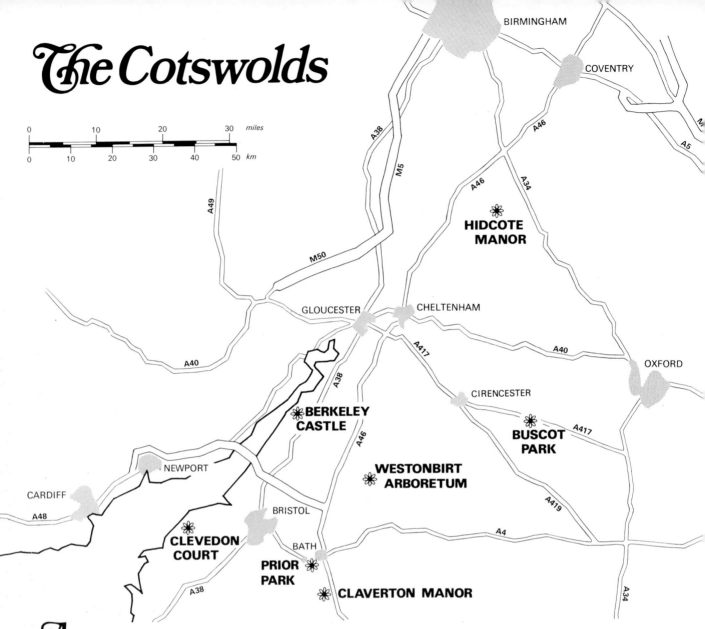

As a range, the Cotswold Hills do not appear very impressive on the map, yet they contain some of the loveliest scenery in England allied to an architecture of almost universally high standard. This outstanding quality of building is in part due to the warm, honey yellow stone of the locality, in part to the happy chance that its period of greatest exploitation coincided with one of the peaks in English culture when the simplicity and dignity of classical styles were predominant. The wool industry brought considerable prosperity to the Cotswolds in the 18th and early 19th centuries. This is reflected in numerous substantial mansions and a string of small towns and large villages all spaciously designed and several with market places of quite exceptional beauty.

Though the hills themselves are limestone, they have many pockets or caps of soil sufficiently rich in humus to produce the moderately acid conditions in which many of the finest exotic trees and shrubs luxuriate. So the Cotswolds have become the site of some of the finest and most famous gardens in the country, particularly of gardens made in the past hundred years. These exploit a rich variety of plants and the theories of picturesque and semi-wild gardening which dominate so much of the early part of this period. They range from almost pure woodland gardens, such as the great arboretum at Westonbirt, to exquisite experiments in the linking of whole series of gardens in miniature, as at Hidcote Manor.

For the purpose of this book I have included in this section the area around Bristol and Bath which, though not strictly in the Cotswold Hills, is adjacent to them and conveniently included in any itinerary which covers them.

Because so many houses and gardens in this area are of modest size they have tended to remain in private ownership and some of the best, from the gardeners' standpoint, are not open to the public sufficiently frequently to be included here. Yet most do open occasionally for charity, and because they are, in general, so lovely it is worth making a special effort to see them.

One of the terrace gardens around Berkeley Castle

Hidcote Manor

Hidcote Bartrim, Gloucestershire. Three miles north-east of Chipping Campden and one mile east of Mickleton off the A46 from Broadway to Stratford-upon-Avon. The National Trust. Open daily, except Tuesdays and Fridays, from April to late October.

This garden was entirely the creation of one man, Major Lawrence Johnston, who was an architect, an artist and a plantsman. All these qualities are displayed in the garden he made from 1905 onwards, and it combines to an unusual degree, and with very great success, formal design, variety of shape and style, and richness of planting, while retaining an overall unity of conception which is the mark of any considerable work of art. Firmness of overall design is combined with numerous changes from large to small enclosures. These are made almost entirely with clipped hedges and are partly necessary to provide shelter because of the very exposed nature of the site, high on the eastern edge of the Cotswold Hills.

The manor house itself, a pleasant old building of Cotswold stone, plays scarcely any part in the design, the long central axis of which is centred at one end on a splendid cedar and at the other on wrought-iron gates leading to the hillside from which extensive views of the countryside can be obtained. Though it is possible to see the whole length of this avenue, it is divided into sections each of which can be fully appreciated only by walking along it. Starting from the cedar one passes through the Old Garden, densely planted in the cottage manner with roses, shrubs and herbaceous plants, into a small circular garden. Then between

borders planted mainly in shades of red, up stone steps and past twin pavilions with a slightly oriental look and so into the Stilt Garden, so called because it is filled by trim hornbeam hedges standing on bare 6-foot high trunks like stilts.

But this is only the beginning of this remarkable garden. Beside the varied and heavily-planted avenue, and entirely self-contained within an encircling hedge of yew, is a great rectangle of grass dominated at one end by two huge beeches on raised ground, and known as The Theatre. This is entirely free of flowering plants as is a second avenue, longer and broader than the main avenue, which runs at right angles from it starting at the pavilions and ending in a second pair of wrought-iron gates. The austerity of these open spaces contrasts dramatically with the lavishness of the planting elsewhere.

This same device is repeated in a series of small gardens tucked into the angles between the main avenue and the Long Walk. There is a pillar garden with rows of yews clipped as columns and small beds filled with a medley of flowers. Another, known as

Mrs Winthrop's Garden, is circular, paved with brick and planted mainly in shades of green and greenish-yellow. A second circular garden, entirely enclosed by a tall yew hedge, contains nothing but grass and leads through a massive archway of yew into a third circle almost entirely filled by a great stone-sided circular pool which is unplanted so that it mirrors the sky and surrounding vegetation. There is a tiny paved garden in the Dutch style with clipped box doves and peacocks, and another little formal garden planted with dwarf hardy fuchsias. Yet a further feature is a rough

cobbled path that leads beside a stream, the banks of which are thickly planted with moisture- and shade-loving plants, including many hardy ferns. Another area, known as the Wilderness, is planted in a random manner with trees and shrubs growing in rough grass. What was once the kitchen garden is now also largely filled with flowers, and even the walls around the entrance yard are covered in climbers. It might be supposed that 50 acres would be required to contain so much variety. In fact the gardens at Hidcote cover no more than 10.

Westonbirt Arboretum

Westonbirt, Gloucestershire. Three miles south-west of Tetbury on the A433 to the A46 and Bath. The Forestry Commission. Open daily throughout the year.

This 80-acre arboretum was started in the mid-19th century as an addition to the garden of Westonbirt House, now a school and entirely separate from it. Over the years it grew into one of the most important private tree collections in England and in 1956 passed into the care of the Forestry Commission.

It is laid out as woodland intersected by wide, straight rides, the sides of which are richly diversified with all manner of exotic trees, deciduous and evergreen. There are also more open glades, one particularly notable because it is surrounded by Japanese maples which give a wonderful display in the autumn. In the main avenue, centred on Westonbirt House, there is a large group of incense cedars (libocedrus), which have now grown to great size and are probably the finest of their kind in the country. Some parts of the arboretum,

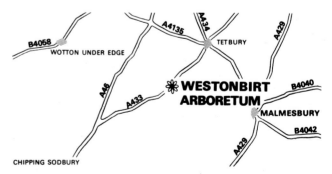

particularly that enclosed by the Circular Drive, have been planned in a more open, park style, with trees and shrubs in irregular groups or planted as isolated specimens, with wide areas of grass between them.

Opposite. The red borders at Hidcote Manor leading to the twin pavilions and the Stilt Garden of hornbeam

Above. Brilliant autumn colour of Japanese maples in the acer glade at Westonbirt Arboretum

Prior Park

Widcombe, Bath, Somerset. One mile southeast of Bath on the road to Claverton. Privately owned. Open on Tuesdays and Wednesdays from May to September, and also on Mondays and Thursdays during August.

Prior Park is a magnificent early 18th-century mansion standing high on one of the hills which overlook Bath from the south. Among gardeners, its fame lies in the fact that it possesses one of the three Palladian bridges built in England during the middle 18th century, the other two being at Wilton House, Wiltshire (see p. 51) and Stowe, Buckinghamshire (see p. 76). In some ways the one at Prior Park is the most spectacularly placed of the trio. It stands at the bottom of the grass slopes below the mansion, where it straddles the first of two small lakes, with the tower of the church of St Thomas à Becket beyond and then the whole panorama of Bath, rising to the Lansdown Ridge. There is another equally dramatic view the other way, across the lakes and the Palladian bridge up the grass slopes, enclosed on each side by woodland, to the great building at the top, which echoes the classical dignity of the bridge, and is built in the same warm-coloured Bath stone.

The panorama and Palladian bridge at Prior Park

Buscot Park

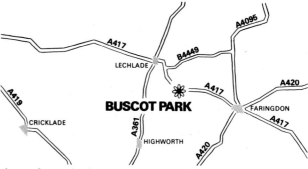

Buscot, Berkshire. Midway between Faringdon and Lechlade on the A417. The National Trust. Open each Wednesday and the first Saturday and subsequent Sunday in each month from April to September, and each Wednesday only from October to March.

The garden is chiefly renowned for the unique canal avenue or alley which links the late 18th-century house with a lake formed at this same period, but it has many other features of interest. The canal walk, designed in the early years of the 20th century by Mr Harold Peto, is entirely formal and for the greater part of its length is flanked with close-trimmed hedges of box and yew. The Adam-style mansion stands on higher ground than the lake, from which it is separated by fairly dense woodland. The avenue passes through this wood, acquiring an almost tunnel-like sense of enclosure and emerging rather dramatically to the bright reflecting surface of the lake. Stone steps lead down from the house terrace to the canal which is then diversified by a series of pools, a fountain and a small stone-balustraded bridge with statues and fastigiate conifers on each side.

The atmosphere is rather that of a 17th-century garden and this is intensified by a number of other formal features, including several quite young tree avenues centred upon or flanked by statues, stone urns and other ornaments. This preoccupation with straight lines and long enclosed vistas even takes in the large walled kitchen garden sited in a hollow through which there is an impressive view to a pavilion on the crest of the far slope.

The canal walk and fountain at Buscot Park

A replica of Washington's garden at Claverton Manor

Claverton Manor

Claverton, Bath, Somerset. Two miles east of Bath off the A36 to Frome. The American Museum in Britain. Open daily, except Mondays, but on all Bank Holidays, from April to mid-October.

The garden of this substantial manor house, built on a hillside overlooking beautifully-wooded country, was a pleasant but unremarkable amalgam of lawns, borders and fine specimen trees. Then the Dames Of America decided to furnish it with a replica of George Washington's little formal flower garden – which formed a part of his considerable garden and estate at Mount Vernon, Virginia – as a feature of the American Museum which has been established at Claverton Manor. This little parterre, with its beds outlined in box, and overlooked by the elegant octagonal pavilion which he used as a study and a schoolroom for his step-children, has transformed it and made it of considerable interest both to garden lovers and to students of garden history. The parterre is divided into two sections, in the smaller of which the beds are long, curving, arranged concentrically and planted with herbaceous perennials and bulbs. In the other section the beds are of various and more elaborate shapes and are planted with old-world roses.

Clevedon Court

Clevedon, Somerset. One mile east of Clevedon on the B3130 to Bristol. The National Trust. Open Sundays, Wednesdays and Thursdays also Bank Holiday Mondays, from April to late September.
This beautiful and very old manor house stands near the foot of a south-facing hill, the upper part of which is densely wooded. The garden lies between the house and the wood and consists of a series of deep terraces, retained in the same grey stone as that of which the manor is built and reached by simple flights of stone stairs. From all the terraces there are fine views across Nailsea Moor towards Weston-super-Mare and Brean Down, and the top terrace is sufficiently high to give an almost plan view of the house below.

There are three garden houses at different levels, one a round castellated building like a squat tower, close to the house; another a domed alcove at the east end of the top terrace, and the third an octagonal building at the western end of the same terrace.

These terraces were much admired by Gertrude Jekyll when she visited Clevedon Court, but the Victorian planting shocked her and she declared in her book *Wall and Water Gardens* that 'the foot of one of the noblest range of terrace walls in England is too good to be given over to the most commonplace forms of bedding'. Present-day visitors will find no such cause for offence for the bedding has gone and in its place is dignified planting with an excellent variety of perennial plants, trees and shrubs which would be entirely to Miss Jekyll's liking.

The well-planted upper terrace terminated by a domed garden room at Clevedon Court

Berkeley Castle

The rectangular water-lily pool on a stone-balustraded terrace at Berkeley Castle

Berkeley, Gloucestershire. In Berkeley on the B4509 from Stone on the A38 Bristol to Gloucester road. Privately owned. Open daily, except Mondays (but on Bank Holiday Mondays), from April to September, also on Sundays only in October.

Berkeley Castle is one of the most romantic and best preserved castles in England, some parts having been built in the 12th century or even earlier. It occupies a position of great natural beauty on the northern side of a wide and shallow valley through which the little Doverte Brook flows. Until the present century the only garden it possessed was a bowling green to the west, and several grass terraces which lapped around the south and east faces of the castle with lovely views of the water meadows below.

The present owner has transformed these terraces by setting many beautiful plants beside them, putting good shrubs and climbers, such as the Glasnevin solanum and *Magnolia delavayi*, to clothe the walls, and making an entirely new formal water garden

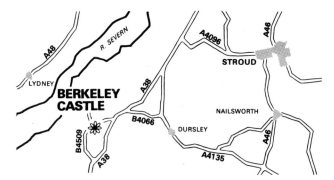

below the bowling green, with a stone summer-house overlooking a rectangular pool filled with water-lilies. From this stone steps lead down to the valley in which a wide area of lawn, with pleasant groupings of trees, shrubs and other plants, gives space from which the castle and the terraces can be viewed.

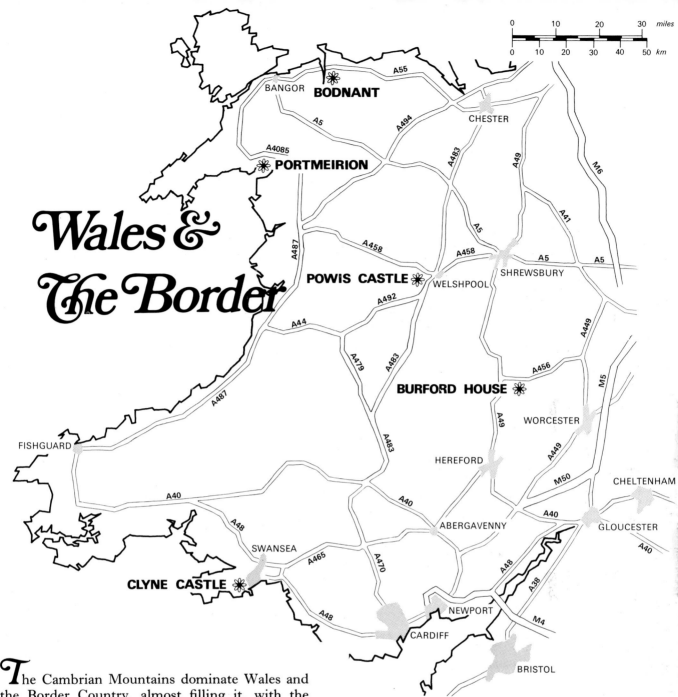

Wales & The Border

The Cambrian Mountains dominate Wales and the Border Country, almost filling it, with the exception of the coastal strip, and developing both in the south and north considerable peaks rivalling, and in the case of Snowdon, exceeding in magnitude those of the Pennine Chain and the Cumbrian Mountains in England.

These mountains and their attendant hills are freely intersected with streams and rivers and in many of the valleys there are fine lakes. Add to this an always interesting and sometimes exceedingly beautiful coastline, abundant trees – in many places growing as forests – a high rainfall and, near the coast, a comparatively mild climate, and one has all the ingredients required for picturesque landscape gardening on a grand scale. Yet with a few notable exceptions Wales lacks gardens of great distinction. Perhaps this is because its wealth has remained strictly confined to the area of the coal-

The view over the Bodnant terraces toward Snowdonia

fields in the south or because of the comparative inaccessibility of much of the interior.

However, there are exceptions to most generalisations and Wales has a particularly brilliant exception all its own. Bodnant in the north is perhaps the greatest British garden made in this century. It is magnificently placed, brilliantly executed and planted with an unsurpassed collection of those plants that have most engaged the attention of modern gardeners.

In the extreme south, at Clyne Castle, is another large collection of exotic trees and shrubs, though it lacks the organisation and the setting that make Bodnant so memorable; while at Powis Castle, close to the western border with England, is the finest example in the British Isles of terracing applied to a site so steep and high that it could fairly be said that the elevation is of greater significance than the plan.

91

Bodnant

Tal-y-cafn, Denbighshire. Four miles south of Colwyn Bay on the A496 to Llanrwst and Betws-y-coed. The National Trust. Open on Tuesdays, Wednesdays, Thursdays, Saturdays and Bank Holiday Mondays from April to October inclusive.

The gardens at Bodnant defy easy classification since they combine features of the Italian formal style, the picturesque landscape, the woodland and the wild, besides containing one of the most comprehensive plant collections in the British Isles. Yet they have been made almost entirely since 1875, though some of the large native trees were planted a century earlier. The site has natural advantages, lying on steeply rising ground on the east side of the River Conway with splendid views to Snowdonia in the south-west and a deep valley of its own through which the little River Hiraethlyn tumbles rapidly to the Conway below.

The ground immediately around the house has been levelled and terraced and, in particular, five terraces have been created on the west side, falling like great steps of unequal depth and width and each planted in a distinctive manner. Thus the top terrace is stone paved and has formal beds of roses; the next is long and narrow and contains a lawn, fountain and a small pool; the third is by far the broadest, flanked by immense cedars and with a large water-lily pool in the middle; the fourth is narrow with patterned brick paths and many roses; and the fifth is the longest, with a simple canal pool down the centre, an open-air stage set in clipped yew at one end and a beautiful early 18th-century Pin Mill used as a garden house at the other. This was brought to its present situation from the Cotswolds in 1938. It is these great terraces which give Bodnant its Italian appearance. They were made between 1905 and 1914 to the design of the 2nd Baron Aberconway, and it is from them that the finest views of the garden, the Conway valley and the distant mountains can be obtained.

Below the terraces is a fine collection of magnolias and, because of the drop in the land, one can look down on their blooms from above. To one side a steep rock garden leads to the valley of the Hiraethlyn, which has been dammed at one point to form a mill pool and waterfall. Here the style becomes natural with many exotic trees now grown to great size, as well as rhododendrons, azaleas and many other shrubs.

From the valley one can ascend by a winding path to the mausoleum, which overlooks it, and then past beds of shrubs and through a little dell garden, with a pool surrounded by *Rhododendron williamsianum,* to more terraced lawns to the south of the house. Here is an attractive circular garden filled with daphnes of all kinds and surrounded by rhododendrons and other shrubs. It is yet one more example of the happy way in which, at Bodnant, formal design has been softened, sometimes almost to the point of obliteration, by the luxuriant planting.

Burford House

Tenbury Wells, Shropshire. One mile west of Tenbury Wells on the A456 from Kidderminster to the A49 south of Ludlow. Privately owned. Open daily May to mid-October.

Burford House is a rather severe brick manor house built in the early 18th century in the wide shallow valley of the little River Ledwych which forms the boundary of its garden. This contains an elegant summer-house built in 1725 and, until the early 1950s, its most notable feature. Since then it has been provided with an entirely new garden in the popular 'glade' style, with island beds and borders of varying shape and size separated by grass paths and wider areas of lawn. Beside the house there is a little raised terrace treated more formally and providing some particularly good views of the garden.

What makes this garden of more than usual interest is the very imaginative use of plants. Trees, shrubs and herbaceous plants are all arranged with very good taste and there are some delightful and unusual combinations, such as the use of clematis to grow through beds of heathers and up columnar forms of cypress and juniper. Though a fairly large garden, much can be learned from it about the use of labour-saving perennial plants and ground cover for smaller gardens where lack of labour and time is important.

Clyne Castle

Swansea, Glamorgan. Between Swansea and Mumbles on the A4067. Swansea Corporation. Open daily throughout the year.

Formerly the home of the late Admiral Sir Vyvyan Heneage Vyvyan, who made a famous collection of rhododendrons and other exotic trees and shrubs here, Clyne Castle was acquired after his death by the Swansea Corporation, and, after suitable alterations had been made, particularly to the paths and other means of access, it was opened as a public park. Nevertheless, it retains much of its original interest as a private garden since most of the original design remains as well as many of the best trees and shrubs.

The castle stands on a spur of high ground which extends to Mumbles Head and commands fine views across Swansea Bay. The garden is largely made on the slopes of this hill and in a considerable valley which cuts through it to the west. Here a stream provides ample scope for planting moisture-loving plants such as candelabra primulas, astilbes, skunk cabbage (lysichitum), rheum and rodgersia, and there is good woodland cover for rhododendrons and azaleas. Many of the large-leaved species thrive in the mild, moist climate of South Wales, and one plantation of *Rhododendron falconeri* has grown to such a size that it completely obscures a little stone tower built by the Admiral so that he might ascend and look down on the great domes of creamy-white blooms.

Near the summit of the hill a small disused quarry provides shelter for some particularly tender plants including *Camellia reticulata*, with immense semi-double rose-pink flowers, and *Rhododendron* Lady Alice Fitzwilliam with spicily-fragrant white flowers.

Opposite. Rhododendrons around the rock garden and stream behind the Pin Mill at Bodnant

Above left. Island beds and columnar cypresses in the modern garden at Burford House. Clematis grow through the heathers and some of the shrubs

Below left. The valley at Clyne Castle through which a stream flows, providing scope for a great variety of planting in an attractively natural style

Portmeirion

Portmadoc, Caernarvonshire. Three miles south-east of Portmadoc off the A497 from Portmadoc to Penrhyndeudraeth. Privately owned. Open daily from Easter to mid-October.

This extraordinary estate was created by Mr Clough Williams-Ellis as an idealised Italian village, complete with church, campanile, villas, inn, piazza and open-air stage. It may be regarded as a charming architectural jest, but it has withstood the test of time and is always fully occupied by permanent residents as well as attracting great numbers of visitors. It is situated on a little promontory jutting out into the sheltered tidal waters of Treath Bach, and there is a constant change of seascape, the estuary at one time being filled with water, at another consisting mainly of wet sand. The village occupies a hollow in the south side of this promontory, and from it woodlands, planted with rhododendrons, azaleas and other colourful exotic shrubs and trees, extend westwards, with many fine views.

In the village itself gardening is mainly ancillary to the main purpose of displaying the colourful architectural features to best advantage, though there are some pleasant effects with yuccas and other sub-tropical plants to heighten the Southern impression, and hydrangeas provide a great deal of summer colour.

Powis Castle

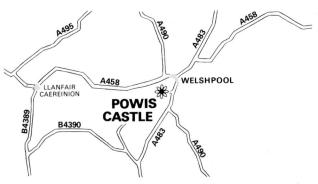

Welshpool, Montgomery. On the south-west side of Welshpool, but cars enter one mile south off the A483 to Newtown. The National Trust. Gardens open daily, except Mondays and Tuesdays, from May to late September. Also open on Spring and Late Summer Bank Holidays.

The castle is a mediaeval building of exceptionally romantic appearance, built of rose-coloured stone and standing on a steep escarpment facing south-east and commanding fine views of the surrounding hills. This escarpment was terraced and planted early in the 18th century; the deep retaining walls match the stone of the castle, though a central section of the first terrace rests on a brick loggia with eight arches which make a prominent feature when seen from below. On these terraces are huge cones cut in yew, and great buttresses of clipped yew, 30 feet high, close in the terraces to the north-east. As a result they are very sheltered and in the present century many slightly tender plants have been established on them. Below the second terrace is an orangery, and on the stone balustrade in front of this are delightful life-size figures of shepherds and shepherdesses cast in lead. A serpentine path, between high yew hedges, leads from these terraces down to the bottom gardens. These are varied, one consisting of a great lawn, another, a former vegetable garden, now turfed over but with the old pyramidal fruit trees remaining as a feature, a third, an entrance garden with elaborate wrought-iron gates and a stone basin and fountain.

The hillside curls around from the south-west of the terraces to enfold the lawn below them and give a gradual descent to the valley near the lower entrance. This spur has been planted as a woodland garden, mainly in the present century, and is known as the Wilderness. It contains many fine trees and shrubs, including rhododendrons and azaleas, and provides some enchanting views of the castle and terraces as well as of the surrounding countryside.

Opposite. A cobbled street in Portmeirion flanked by hydrangeas which give added colour to a gay scene

Above. Powis Castle and its steeply terraced gardens as seen from the much newer woodland garden which sweeps in a great horse-shoe around it

Right. Lead figures of shepherds and shepherdesses on the stone balustrade above the orangery, which is built into one of the terraces at Powis Castle

95

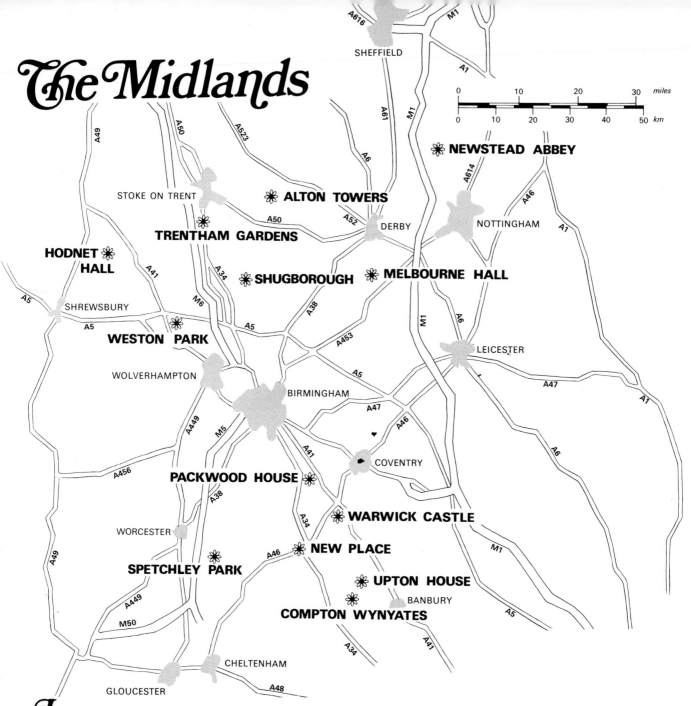

The Midlands

It might be supposed that the wealth produced by the industrialisation of vast areas from Coventry to Wolverhampton, and further north in the Potteries and around Burton-on-Trent and Derby, would have determined the character of the great gardens of this area, but this is far from being the case. Long before the industrial revolution, this was a prosperous part of Britain with good farms, fine houses and imposing castles. Warwick Castle has been described as one of the most authentically mediaeval in the country, yet it is less than 10 miles from the heart of Coventry. Packwood House, a lovely 16th-century timber-framed building with an even more remarkable 17th-century topiary garden, is now almost sandwiched between the expanding suburbs of Coventry and Birmingham. Yet it miraculously retains a rural seclusion almost as great as it enjoyed when it was first built by William Fetherston, who was described as a yeoman of sufficient wealth to contribute towards the preparations against the Spanish Armada. A little further south, Compton Wynyates boasts a building even more venerable and romantic, though its topiary garden is a modern reconstruction and not a genuine antique.

On the southern edge of Derbyshire, Melbourne Hall in structure and garden remains a monument to the taste of the 17th and 18th-century gentry, but the Gothic was to return in even more exuberant abandon and is seen at its zenith at Alton Towers near Uttoxeter, a house and garden on which fabulous wealth was expended in the early 19th century. The house is now largely a romantic ruin, but the garden is preserved and has been even further diversified.

The wrought-iron arbour at Melbourne Hall

Spetchley Park

Spetchley, Worcestershire. Three miles east of Worcester on the A422 road to Alcester. Privately owned. Open on Sundays, Saturdays, and also on Bank Holiday Mondays and the following Tuesdays, from April to September.

Gardening has been carried on at Spetchley Park for something like 300 years, but what the visitor sees to-day is very largely a Reptonian landscape including a large lake, laid out at about the time the present house was built in 1820, to which many later features have been added. These include the planting of fine trees as specimens (this is being continued at the present time), and a fascinating series of formal gardens enclosed by yew hedges, but planted most informally with a variety of herbaceous plants, shrubs and even small trees, some of which have now outgrown their site.

In their variety of styles and planting material the gardens mirror the change of fashion over the best part of two centuries. The formal gardens, with their delightful little lead statues and fountain playing into an elaborate stone basin, were made in the 19th century but look back to an earlier period. A great deal of the rich planting which characterises Spetchley Park is of the present century, but it is possible that some of the very large cedars were planted before 1680 when John Evelyn visited Spetchley Park and commented on newly-planted conifers from the Mediterranean. It is also of interest that the river-like extension of the lake, which separates the lawns and the shrubberies around the house from the main part of the garden, is the remains of a moat, which once partly surrounded an Elizabethan house destroyed by fire after the battle of Worcester.

Melbourne Hall

Melbourne, Derbyshire. At Melbourne, seven miles south of Derby on the A514 to Swadlincote, Privately owned. Open daily, except Mondays and Fridays, from early July to late September, Sundays only from April to June, and Easter, Spring and Late Summer Bank Holidays.

This is one of the best preserved gardens of modest size of the 17th and early 18th centuries. The famous London nursery firm, London and Wise, had a hand in making it, and both they and the owner, Thomas Coke, were influenced by the work of Le Nôtre in France.

The garden is roughly L-shaped and falls into two interlinked parts. To the east of the house, where the land falls gently and then rises again, large rectangular terraces have been made leading down to a formal lake, known as the Great Basin, on the far side of which stands an elaborate pavilion of partly gilded wrought-iron. Beyond this a wide avenue through woodland permits a view of the far hilltop.

The second section, made a little later, leads away from the Great Basin to the right as one looks at it from the house. Here the ground rises again and much of it is thickly planted with trees through which numerous avenues have been cut. The main avenue is broken by two large circular pools with fountains, and leads up to a large circle of grass from which more avenues radiate and in the centre of which is an enormous lead urn representing the four seasons.

Other features of this remarkable garden are a great

tunnel of yew, a stone dovecot transformed into a muniment room, a grotto and numerous statues some, such as those representing cherubs quarrelling and then making friends again, of great charm.

Warwick Castle

Warwick, Warwickshire. In Warwick. Privately owned. Open daily throughout the year except for December.

It is difficult to-day to determine how much of what one sees at Warwick Castle can be attributed to Brown, and how much has been added by later hands. There are pleasant groupings of trees interspersed by areas of grass, one in the middle distance very large and open, perhaps serving a similar scenic role to that accorded to water in later compositions. The whole is overlooked by a large orangery placed behind a series of curving terraces with a large, circular stone basin for water-lilies centrally placed, and the parterre beds neatly outlined in box and decorated with topiary work. This is a story-book castle, magnificently towered and battlemented and mounted on the edge of a cliff overhanging the Avon. It occupies a key position in Warwick, itself a romantic and still partially-walled town, and it attracts visitors in their thousands from all parts of the world.

To those who are garden minded there is an additional interest in the garden, which is said to have been the first to be 'landscaped' by Lancelot Brown. What he achieved in the limited space at his disposal cannot be compared with his later masterpieces, but it was sufficient to bring him to the notice of Horace Walpole, who said that 'it is well laid out by one Brown who has set up on a few ideas of Kent and Mr Southcote'.

Trentham Gardens

Trentham, Staffordshire. Three-and-a-half miles south of Stoke on Trent on A34. Privately owned. Open daily throughout the year except for Christmas Day.

For 150 years Trentham was one of the great houses of Britain. Originally designed by Lancelot Brown in the second half of the 18th century, it was afterwards considerably enlarged and elaborated in the mid-19th century by Sir Charles Barry. Almost all this has now been razed to the ground, but the great gardens, made to complement the building, remain and are now an amusement park. The loss of the building is serious, depriving the gardens of their *raison d'être*, yet they continue to have a considerable interest and beauty of their own. There are, in fact, two separate gardens, one in the landscape style made around a huge lake originally created by Lancelot Brown by widening the River Trent, but now fed from clean hillside streams since the river water had become foul; the second, a garden in the Italian style, made by Sir Charles Barry and W. A. Nesfield when the house was enlarged and a more formal garden was required.

The lake, nearly a mile in length, is partly enfolded by the Tittensor Hills. It is of great beauty and the woods which almost surround it have been well underplanted with a variety of exotic shrubs. At one time this 'natural' style of gardening must have continued right to the house, but, during the 19th-century development, the whole of the area between lake and house was converted into a formal garden on the Italian pattern with a raised balustraded terrace immediately

in front of the house. This served as a vantage point from which to look down on the elaborate pattern of flower beds in the parterre below. Statues, urns, ornaments and some handsome stone pavilions decorate this garden, the main vista of which is terminated at the lakeside by a large statue of Perseus. The whole effect, with the great length of water beyond disappearing behind an island and with pleasure boats plying upon it, is rather that of an unusually fine and broad esplanade at a popular seaside resort.

Opposite top. Charming lead figures which stand in the formal gardens at Spetchley Park

Opposite bottom. The Great Basin, formal terraces and Melbourne Hall seen from Robert Bakewell's arbour

Below. Trentham Gardens looking across the elaborate Italian terraces to Lancelot Brown's landscape

Upton House

Edge Hill, Warwickshire. One mile south of Edge Hill on A422 from Banbury to Stratford-upon-Avon. The National Trust. Open on Wednesdays and Saturdays from July to September, and on Wednesdays only from October to June.

This late 17th-century house stands on high ground and the land falls steeply into a narrow valley. Full use of this natural feature has been made to create what are, in effect, two quite distinct gardens. From the house the visitor steps on to a level lawn enclosed on each side by trees and apparently leading directly to a wide avenue of trees disappearing into the distance. It is only on crossing the lawn that the valley which separates it from this distant landscape prospect is revealed. In the bottom is a long river-like lake, and on the near slope a series of steep, flower-covered terraces followed by a large sloping kitchen garden. Flights of stone steps lead down from terrace to terrace. On one side of the kitchen garden a grass walk flanked by double herbaceous borders completes the descent to the lake, and on the other the path runs by two small enclosed gardens.

The surprises are not yet over, for, on turning right, further gardens are revealed. First, one of ornamental cherries made in the drained site of a former lake, and then a delightful water and bog garden intersected with streams and pools and densely planted with foliage and flowering plants.

Compton Wynyates

Banbury, Warwickshire. Eight miles west of Banbury between the villages of Tysoe and Winderton. Privately owned. Open on Wednesdays, Saturdays and Bank Holidays from April to September and also on Sundays from June to August.

The house is one of the most romantically-beautiful examples of early 16th-century architecture. It is built of a warm pink stone and has been as lovingly restored inside as it has out. The place was once known as Compton-in-the-Hole, which graphically indicates the steep-sided nature of the hollow or 'coombe' in which it lies, though it does scant justice to its natural beauty.

Because of its situation, the house can be viewed from above, particularly on the east and south sides, and it was possibly this fact, rather than any intention to imitate the styles of 16th- or 17th-century gardening, that led the 5th Marquess of Northampton in 1895 to plan the garden to the south on strictly formal lines. He christened it the Best Garden and he laid it out in four large rectangular beds edged with box and containing topiary specimens, two at each corner and four in the centre. The beds were filled with herbaceous plants, but in time the topiary grew up and took sufficient command of the scene for most of the herbaceous plants to be removed and the rectangles to be grassed over, except for a narrow border around each maintaining the original pattern. All this is most fortunate, for to-day these specimens, grown to maturity, clipped to elaborate shapes and backed by massive clipped hedges of yew, provide a perfect setting for the building, entirely in character with its appearance and period.

The area immediately around the house has been kept clear and is occupied in the main by lawns, but on the west, projecting into the sole remaining part of the moat which once encircled the building, a pleasant formal garden has been planted mainly with roses and peonies. On the surrounding slopes, around the neighbouring church and at the approaches to the house, fine ornamental trees have been established, and the walls themselves have been used to shelter or support a variety of exotic climbers and other plants.

New Place

Stratford-upon-Avon, Warwickshire. In Chapel Street, Stratford-upon-Avon. The Shakespeare Birthplace Trust. Open on weekdays throughout the year and also on Sundays from April to October.

Along half the length of New Street are three little gardens, side by side, that attract a great many visitors, particularly in summer when they are at their gayest. One shows the foundations of Shakespeare's last home, New Place, and is mainly lawns with a few shrubs and rock plants. The second is laid out as an Elizabethan knot garden, a sunken square completely surrounded by a raised walk and a hedge and filled with patterned beds, edged with box, and planted with the gayest medley of flowers in season. The third is the largest and is known as the Great Garden of New Street. It has a large lawn with seats and some good trees, including a mulberry and, along the far boundary from the road, a line of chestnut trees, but what makes it so very distinctive are its twin flower borders divided into compartments with box hedges trimmed to different heights and patterns. All three gardens are always well maintained.

Opposite top. Ornamental rheums and other moisture-loving plants in the streamside garden, Upton House

Opposite bottom. Elaborately-clipped topiary specimens at Compton Wynyates

Above. The west front at Compton Wynyates seen in spring through a screen of Japanese Cherries

Below. The brilliantly-planted knot garden in New Place, Shakespeare's last home in Stratford-upon-Avon

Hodnet Hall

Hodnet, Shropshire. Six miles south-east of Market Drayton on the A442 between Wellington and Whitchurch. Privately owned. Open daily from April to early October.

Garden making began at Hodnet Hall in 1922 and has been continued almost without break to the present day. The garden, about 50 acres in extent, lies along a shallow valley which has been dammed at various levels to form a chain of lakes. Planning is, in the main, informal, in the 20th-century woodland and water style, but the planting around the lower lakes is on exceptionally bold lines with great drifts of astilbes, primulas, rhododendrons, azaleas and other plants. At some seasons the display is almost as massed and colourful as in a garden stocked with bedding plants. There are fine collections of camellias, magnolias, flowering cherries, hydrangeas and Japanese maples as well as of trees and shrubs of many other kinds.

Around the building a more formal style has been adopted and there is a simple rose garden surrounded by a yew hedge. A terrace in front of the house commands fine views of several of the lakes and the country on the far side of the valley with, in the middle distance, a large stone dovecot built in the mid-17th century, making a good eye-catcher. So does a huge boulder of granite, said to be of glacial origin, which has been placed in a prominent position nearer to the house. Wide steps, flanked by thickly planted beds of heathers, rhododendrons, barberries, rose species and other shrubs, lead down from this terrace to the lake in front of the house.

There are many other features in this varied and richly stocked garden, including a large circular rose and peony garden made in a sheltered sandstone pit.

Packwood House

Hockley Heath, Warwickshire. One mile east of Hockley Heath off the B4439 to Warwick. The National Trust. Open on Tuesdays, Wednesdays, Thursdays, Saturdays and Bank Holidays from April to September, and on Wednesdays, Saturdays and Bank Holidays from October to March.

Though the gardens at Packwood House are generally thought of in terms of their extraordinary topiary specimens representing the Sermon on the Mount, there are, in fact, three gardens adjacent to one another and their contrast in style and texture contributes largely to the effectiveness of the whole scheme. Immediately to the south of the house is a rectangular mid-17th-century garden, walled in brick, with four elegant brick pavilions, one at each corner. The space is open and flat except for a simple canal pool in an area sunk below the general level.

The second garden lies beyond and is reached by semi-circular steps and early 18th-century wrought-iron gates. This is the topiary garden filled with immense cones of trimmed yews representing 'the multitude' and leading to a mount on which stands a solitary specimen, 'the Master', with 'the apostles'

and 'the evangelists' clustered in front and ranged on each side. The whole was devised in the latter half of the 17th century by John Fetherston, who could scarcely have conceived the dramatic effect now made by these dark, crowded, vertical shapes, grown to such mammoth proportions.

To complete this study in contrasts, to one side a large informal lake has been formed in the 18th-century landscape style, the silver surface of which is unbroken by plant or island and serves only to reflect the surrounding trees, the dark shapes of the yews and the beautiful old building itself.

Newstead Abbey

Nottingham, Nottinghamshire. Nine miles north of Nottingham on the A60 to Mansfield. Nottingham Corporation. Gardens open daily throughout the year.

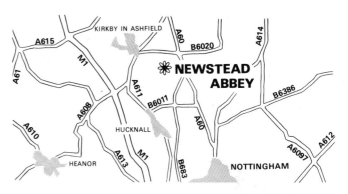

Parts of Newstead Abbey are very old and gardening has undoubtedly gone on there for hundreds of years, though much of the garden as it is seen to-day has been created during the 19th and 20th centuries. It became a house in 1540 and was subsequently the home of the Byrons for 250 years. However, the large Garden Lake which lies to the south of the house was not made until the early 19th century after the poet Byron had sold the estate. The even larger Upper Lake, situated to the south-east, is far older, and was used in the 18th century by the 5th Lord Byron for mock battles in various ships which he kept on the lake for this purpose. Water from the Garden Lake now overflows into an elaborate Japanese garden with streams, water-loving plants, conifers and Japanese stone ornaments, and this was an early 20th-century addition.

Between the Garden Lake and the Abbey there is a rectangular, mediaeval fish pond and to the north and east there are formal gardens, some features of which are also very old. The central feature here is a large rectangular pool, the Eagle Pond, sunk deeply with

grassed terraces and wide lawns around it. The lawns are themselves surrounded by a raised walk against the outer walls of the garden, supported in part by 14th-century buttresses. But a complex parterre, with geometric beds enclosed in clipped box, which separates this part of the garden from the abbey, is much more recent.

There are two rose gardens, the larger of which has been made recently in what was once the kitchen garden and is still surrounded by a high brick wall. The rock garden is extensive, but, like so many such 19th-century constructions, is more suitable for the cultivation of small shrubs and herbaceous plants than of genuine mountain plants. There are also plantations of azaleas and rhododendrons.

Opposite left. Some of the lakes which make the garden of Hodnet Hall so remarkable. All are well planted

Opposite right. 'The multitude' represented in huge specimens of clipped yew at Packwood House

Below. Newstead Abbey seen across the Garden Lake which provides it with a lovely landscape setting

Alton Towers

Alton, Staffordshire. Four miles east of Cheadle off the B5032 between Cheadle and Mayfield. Owned by a private company which runs part of the grounds as an amusement park. Open daily from Good Friday to early October.

This extraordinary and beautiful garden is an outstanding example of early 19th-century exuberance in producing 'picturesque' landscape. It was commenced about 1814 by the 15th Earl of Shrewsbury, who planned it as a suitably romantic setting for the great neo-Gothic building which had been, at least in part, designed for him by A. W. Pugin. The site is a steep-sided valley through which a stream flows. Into this naturally beautiful setting a large number of buildings and ornaments were introduced, among them an elaborate Chinese pagoda standing in a lake and spouting a great column of water from its summit; a Chinese temple, high on the hillside and commanding a splendid view of the garden and house; elaborate conservatories, a colonnade and a curious stone fountain with a screw-like pattern.

There is a large rock garden with cascades and from a bridge above this a panoramic view of the valley can be obtained. Many fine trees and shrubs have been planted on the slopes, cedars, copper beeches and fern-leaved beech being particularly noteworthy. Around the conservatory and colonnade the design is more formal with considerable bedding out and a large rose garden well stocked with many, colourful up-to-date varieties.

The 15th Earl of Shrewsbury died in 1827 and the garden was completed by his son John, the 16th Earl. It is said that by the time he died in 1852 more than a million pounds had been spent on the garden. Time has mellowed what must originally have been an over-elaborate conception with little cohesive design to give it unity, and to-day its many features have been absorbed into a landscape which is sufficiently large and heavily wooded to carry them without offence. In return they give it an interest in detail lacking in some better organised designs and also provide objects of continuing fascination.

Weston Park

Weston under Lizard, Shropshire. At Weston under Lizard five miles east of Oakengates on the A5 to Brownhills. Privately owned. Open on Wednesdays, Thursdays, Saturdays and Sundays from May to early September and also on Bank Holiday weekends.

The garden at Weston Park has been made and extended over a period of 300 years and is a fine example of the successful integration of both formal and landscape ideals in garden planning. The park to the south and the woodland to the east are the work of Lancelot Brown and are remarkably well preserved. The land falls away gently, allowing a fine view of the large lake, which was Brown's accustomed way of filling the middle distance of his landscapes, and the various clumps and belts of trees are well disposed to carry the eye to this lake and suitably diversify the view.

Another lake is concealed in the woodland, a much more mysterious place with a little domed temple looking across to a stone bridge. Paths wind through the trees to a rustic cottage in a clearing at the far end. On the southern edge of the wood, in full view of the house, is a handsome orangery, designed by James Paine at the time that Brown was laying out the landscape, and known as the Temple of Diana because the room behind it is decorated with panels depicting the exploits of that Greek goddess. Immediately to the south of the house is a garden of a very different character, a series of terraces, one with an elaborate parterre, two more with flower beds of simpler pattern, a fourth quite plain and thrust out in a great bow front into Brown's park. Another orangery, added in 1865, extends the line of the house to the west, and, with the church behind it, backs the most elaborately-patterned terrace. Together these terraces provide a firm and dignified setting for the house and a series of elegant platforms from which to view the Brownian landscape.

Shugborough

Great Haywood, Staffordshire. Five-and-a-half miles south-east of Stafford on A513 to Rugeley. Entrance at Milford. The National Trust and Staffordshire County Council. Open daily except Mondays (but on Bank Holiday Mondays) from late March to late October.

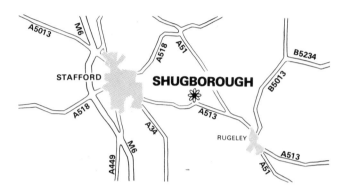

This fine 18th-century mansion stands beside the little River Sow, where it joins the River Trent. To the south are the well-wooded slopes of Cannock Chase; in all a landscape which required little 'improvement'. The Ansons (including the famous Admiral) who made the garden had only to plant more trees and erect a number of interesting buildings, monuments and 'ruins', to achieve their end, and it is these which give it much of its period charm today. A later generation actually created a new course for the river, leaving the old river dammed and still and purely decorative. In the 19th century the well-known garden designer W. A. Nesfield made a series of wide, shallow terraces between the house and the river. Much additional planting was also carried out and this is being renewed or added to at the present time. The cedars are particularly fine and there is one immense yew which covers about a quarter of an acre.

Opposite. The Chinese pagoda fountain at Alton Towers is one of the many elaborate buildings which can be found in this most unusual garden

Top right. The formal terraces at Weston Park with their gay summer bedding provide an interesting contrast to Lancelot Brown's lake and woodland landscape garden which can be seen in the distance

Bottom right. The elegant Chinese House at Shugborough has ornamental lattice-work over the windows and was built in 1747, and the iron bridge was added in 1813. These are characteristic of a number of interesting features which have been constructed in many parts of this garden

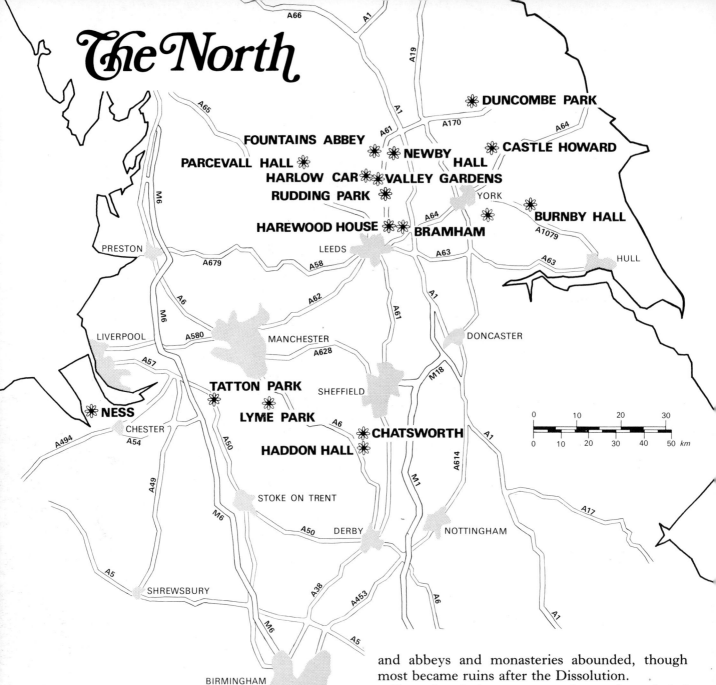

The North

DUNCOMBE PARK

FOUNTAINS ABBEY

PARCEVALL HALL

NEWBY HALL

CASTLE HOWARD

HARLOW CAR — VALLEY GARDENS

RUDDING PARK

HAREWOOD HOUSE

BRAMHAM

BURNBY HALL

YORK

LEEDS

PRESTON

LIVERPOOL

MANCHESTER

DONCASTER

TATTON PARK

SHEFFIELD

NESS

LYME PARK

CHESTER

CHATSWORTH

HADDON HALL

STOKE ON TRENT

DERBY

NOTTINGHAM

HULL

SHREWSBURY

BIRMINGHAM

The second great concentration of industry in England extends from Liverpool in the west to Hull in the east and includes such great cities as Manchester, Sheffield and Leeds. Even more than the industry of the Midlands, it is based on coalfields, the largest in area in the British Isles.

In the field of gardening another parallel may be drawn between this area and the Midlands. Here, too, the wealth of industry is only partly responsible for the many great gardens that abound, many of which were created long before coal had become important and industry had commenced to expand.

For Yorkshire, England's largest county, which covers so much of this area, has been the home of great noblemen for many centuries. Barons fought their battles here in feudal times and their descendants built splendid mansions to replace the outmoded castles. The church was strong here, too,

and abbeys and monasteries abounded, though most became ruins after the Dissolution.

But what is important to the garden-minded visitor is that many of these Yorkshire noblemen and gentry turned to the more peaceful arts of gardening and practised them with exceptional skill and originality. Some of them, like John Aislabie at Studley Royal and Thomas Duncombe at Duncombe Park, derived a part of their inspiration from the lovely ruins of abbeys that adjoined their estates. Others, such as the Earl of Carlisle at Castle Howard and Lord Bingley at Bramham, set off on lines of their own, and yet others called in the help of professionals, so that there seems to be scarcely a garden landscape in Yorkshire that is not ascribed in some measure to Lancelot Brown or his pupils.

The tradition has continued to the present day, for at Harlow Car, Parcevall Hall or even in the parks of Harrogate will be found gardens that are as original as they are exciting and delightful.

The central glade and urn at Rudding Park

Burnby Hall

Pocklington, Yorkshire. In Pocklington, twelve miles east of York on the B1246 from Barmby Moor to Great Driffield. Pocklington Rural District Council. Open daily from April to October.

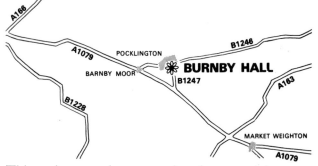

One of the two great lakes at Burnby Hall made for a unique collection of water-lilies

This unique garden was privately created between 1903 and 1910 for the main purpose of growing a great collection of hardy water-lilies. When its owner died he left it to the local council which now uses the house as offices and maintains the garden as a public amenity. A small charge is made for admission during the water-lily season.

To accommodate the collection two large lakes were constructed in concrete. These are at different levels and are connected by a stream flowing through a rock garden which also flanks the pools for a considerable distance and provides a subsidiary feature of great interest. Upper Water is 205 yards long and 70 yards wide at its greatest measurement, and Lower Water 110 yards long and 30 yards wide. Both have been shaped with so much skill and their edges concealed so well with reeds, rushes, gunneras, ferns and other marginal plants that they appear entirely natural. In all, something like 60 different varieties of water-lily are grown in every available colour and arranged in great drifts of a kind for maximum effect. Lawns broken by flower beds separate the house from Upper Water and trees and shrubs enclose the whole garden.

Haddon Hall

Bakewell, Derbyshire. Two miles south of Bakewell on the A6 to Matlock. Privately owned. Open daily, except on Sundays and Mondays, from April to September.

Some parts of Haddon Hall were built in the 12th century, but additions and alterations continued until the early 17th century, so that the building is a compendium of architectural styles over a period of about 500 years.

The site of the house is dramatically placed on an escarpment overlooking the River Wye and the terraced gardens have been cut out of this steep slope. Architecturally, they have considerable beauty and interest, the lowest and deepest terrace being retained by an enormous buttressed wall of rough-hewn stone, and those higher up being bounded by handsome stone balustrades. Wide stone steps, also with stone balustrades, link two of these terraces and the whole makes a pleasing progression to the eye.

A great deal of planting has been carried out on these terraces in the present century, largely with roses, so that it is in summer that the gardens make their most spectacular effect. Good hardy plants, shrubs and climbers have also been used and, on the lower buttressed wall, great drifts of aubrieta which contribute greatly to the spring display.

The terraces provide a good vantage point from which there are fine views of the River Wye and of the ancient stone bridge over which it is said that Dorothy Vernon eloped from the castle to marry John Manners, the son of the Earl of Rutland.

Harlow Car

Harrogate, Yorkshire. One mile west of Harrogate off the A59 to Skipton. The Northern Horticultural Society. Open daily throughout the year.

Left. Roses growing on one of the upper terraces at Haddon Hall, where the fine stonework is a feature

Right. One of the beautiful rock gardens at Harlow Car, garden of the Northern Horticultural Society

The making of this garden began shortly after the Second World War, and it is still being extended. It was planned primarily as a trial ground for the north of England and trial beds of various plants still take up a considerable amount of ground, but as the garden has been enlarged it has become increasingly ornamental in character. It occupies a shallow valley through which flows a stream containing one of the medicinal waters for which Harrogate is famous. An old pump house beside this stream has been converted for use as a library, rest room and offices for the Northern Horticultural Society.

The banks of the stream have been heavily planted with a variety of moisture-loving plants including candelabra primulas and astilbes. On one side, peat beds have been built for lime-hating plants and on the other a series of large, well-constructed rock gardens and rock beds accommodate an exceptionally fine collection of alpines. Thin woodland beyond the stream provides cover for a considerable collection of rhododendrons and other shade-loving shrubs, while on the open slope to the east are extensive shrub and herbaceous borders, a well-planned rose garden and borders of annuals. The standard of planning, planting and maintenance throughout is high, and this is a garden which generously repays visiting at any time in the varied gardening year.

Harewood House

Harewood, Yorkshire. Seven miles north of Leeds on the A61 to Harrogate. Privately owned. Open daily from Easter Saturday to September and on Sundays only in October.

This is one of the great houses of Yorkshire, attributed in part to Robert Adam, 18th century, and in part to Sir Charles Barry in the mid-19th century. Lancelot Brown was engaged to landscape the garden, but the two large stone-balustraded terraces in front of the house are the work of Sir Charles Barry, and are typical of the Victorian desire for greater opulence and formality and for a place in which to grow flowering plants. To-day the elaborate Victorian bedding has been replaced by a much simpler and more easily maintained rose garden.

It is in the valley below that Lancelot Brown's work appears and, since there has been less of the later planting and embellishment characteristic of so many 18th-century landscape gardens, it is probably to-day much as he intended it. In the bottom of the valley is a large lake formed by damming a stream but it is only partly visible from the terraces above as sections of it are screened by trees and the natural contours of the land. Only by descending the hillside and moving around the valley are the full beauties of this landscape revealed. One particularly deep dell has been filled with primulas, a recent innovation.

Lyme Park

Cheshire. Quarter-of-a-mile west of Disley on the A6 from Whaley Bridge to Stockport. The National Trust and Stockport Corporation. Garden open daily throughout the ear.

The mansion stands on a spur of ground in rugged moorland, and in order to form level terraces to west and south it was necessary to move a great deal of soil and build buttressed retaining walls, in places as much as 20 feet high. This work was done in the 17th century before the building was largely redesigned in the Palladian manner by Giacomo Leoni. In the process a level rectangle of land was formed beneath the walls and was laid out as a formal garden with central pool and fountain and an assortment of geometric beds. There is nothing very novel about this parterre except its situation within the angle of these very high walls, so that from the terraces it can be viewed almost vertically from above. The beds and the planting have been simplified to meet the labour requirements of the 20th century, otherwise this fascinating little garden remains much as it was when created nearly 300 years ago.

Other features at Lyme Park are a small informal lake to the south of the mansion, made long before the fashion for such landscape features, and an orangery

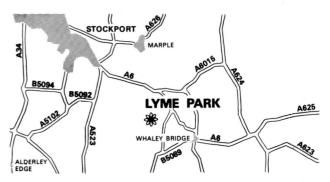

on a raised terrace to the east of the house which was not built until the early 19th century but, at least in part, follows designs by Leoni and so harmonises very well with the main building.

Above. Brown's 18th-century landscape viewed from Barry's 19th-century terraces at Harewood House

Opposite top. The Four Faces urn and alleys at Bramham before the storm of 1962 destroyed many trees

Opposite bottom. The Dutch Garden at Lyme Park

Bramham

Bramham, Yorkshire. Four miles south of Wetherby and eight miles east of Leeds, off the road between Bramham and Leeds. Privately owned. Open on Sundays and Bank Holidays (Monday and Tuesday) from Easter Sunday to September.

Until a night in February, 1962, Bramham Park was one of the finest examples in the British Isles of the late 17th-century French style of garden making – the style, so often associated with the name of Le Nôtre, in which long and radiating avenues are cut through a dense cover of woodland and are embellished with various architectural features, such as canals, pools, fountains, temples and statuary. On that night a gale of unprecedented violence swept the county and destroyed more than 200 of the fine old beeches at Bramham, besides doing a great deal of damage to the undergrowth. What remains is no more than a ghost of the former splendour, though extensive replanting has been carried out, and, in time, the great avenues will take shape again.

Yet Bramham still has its beauties. Around the house there are some charming small gardens which show no trace of the havoc caused by the gale, and the daffodils lavishly naturalised in the woodlands still bloom as freely each spring. The skeleton of the original design can still be seen clearly and the various buildings and waterworks remain, and are being repaired. For the imaginative visitor with some knowledge of garden history, there is even considerable interest in that these sparsely-furnished avenues represent what must have been seen by many 17th- and 18th-century garden makers during most of their life-times, for, unless natural woodland existed through which to cut their avenues, they must of necessity have waited many years for their newly-planted trees to grow up.

Duncombe Park

Helmsley, Yorkshire. Respectively one mile west of Helmsley from the A170 to Thirsk and two miles north-west of Helmsley on the B1257 to Stokesley. Privately owned. Duncombe Park is open on Wednesdays from May to August, and Rievaulx Terrace is open daily throughout the year.

These two gardens must be considered together since, though separate, they form part of the same conception: to provide the best possible viewpoints of the beautiful valley of the River Rye and its surrounding hills.

For this especial purpose Duncombe Park was first provided with a great curving grass terrace around the rim of the hill on which the mansion stands. The terrace, half-a-mile long and backed by woodland, is devoid of ornament except for a classical temple at each end and, in the middle where it is linked to the house, a large statue of Father Time. At the south end the terrace turns sharply west to follow the line of the hill, but there is no further ornamentation. The whole conception is so severe in its simplicity that some visitors may not even regard it as a garden. Yet it was an undoubted prototype of the landscape style which was to follow and to become so popular in the 18th century.

Its counterpart, the Rievaulx Terrace, was made more than 40 years later when that great movement in English garden making was already in full swing. It was constructed by the grandson of Thomas Duncombe, who made the first terrace, and its purpose was to capture in a similar manner the superb view of the ruined Cistercian monastery, Rievaulx Abbey, further up the valley.

This second terrace has been built with many of the features of the Duncombe Park terrace, but since there is no house adjacent to it there is no lawn and no figure corresponding to Father Time. But the two classical buildings are repeated, one at each end of its half-a-mile length, a domed temple to the south-east similar to that at the south end of the Duncombe terrace, but to the north-west is a larger, rectangular temple with a columned portico in the Palladian style. The terrace is backed by a thick belt of trees and more trees grow on the slopes below, but they are not permitted to get to such a height that they obscure the distant landscape, and wide gaps are maintained through them to channel one enchanting view after another of the picturesque ruins of Rievaulx Abbey which are situated below.

Opposite top. View southwards along the broad sweep of the grass terrace at Duncombe Park. The Doric temple stands at the south-east corner of the terrace where it turns sharply to follow the line of the hill

Tatton Park

Knutsford, Cheshire. Two miles north of Knutsford off the A556 just north of its junction with the M6. The National Trust. Open daily, except Mondays, but on all Bank Holiday Mondays, from April to mid-October.

There has been development in the gardens of Tatton Park for about 200 years. It is all said to have begun with Lancelot Brown who may have had something to do with the planning of the 200-acre park in the mid-18th century. What is more certain is that Humphrey Repton made many improvements to this landscape in the early 1790s; while in the early years of the 19th century, a tall and narrow temple in the Grecian style was erected at the end of a broad walk which runs right through the gardens to the ha-ha separating it from the park. Towards the middle of that century the fine stone-balustraded terraces and parterres were made in front of the house. Tradition has it that they were the work of Sir Joseph Paxton and they are certainly of a style and quality of which he would have approved. The handsome orangery, standing near the Georgian mansion, is the work of Lewis Wyatt in about 1811 when the house was nearing completion. Beside it is a large Victorian fernhouse in which there are some mature specimens of the New Zealand tree ferns.

Not much more seems to have happened at Tatton Park until the present century when a great deal of additional planting and garden making has been carried out. Large numbers of exotic trees and shrubs have been established. There are banks and coppices of rhododendrons and azaleas which make a great display in spring and early summer. At the farthest part of the garden from the house, there is a large lake with an island on which a Japanese Shinto temple has been built, reached by a half-moon Japanese bridge. Nearby, around a smaller pool, there is a delightful little garden in the Japanese style with stone ornaments and lanterns.

Indeed the garden of Tatton Park is full of unexpected features, such as an African hut standing among the trees near an intersection of paths; several small pools with statues or fountains; an ancient tower used by sheepwatchers to guard the flocks in the park, and, hard by it, a little formal rose garden hidden away behind immense and elaborately-trimmed yew hedges.

Opposite bottom. This delightful small Japanese temple and graceful half-moon bridge are two of the many unusual and interesting features which can be seen in the gardens at Tatton Park

Newby Hall

Skelton, West Riding of Yorkshire. Three miles north-west of Boroughbridge, and three miles south-east of Ripon on a minor road that links these two towns via Skelton. Privately owned. Open daily from Easter Saturday to mid-October.

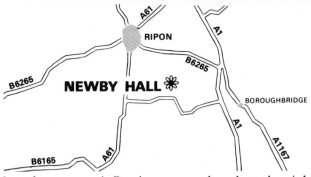

The house, originally built in the early 17th century, was considerably altered later in the century by Robert Adam. The garden has a classical firmness of outline to match the formal dignity of the building, but was probably not started until the late 19th century, and has been very largely made in the last 40 years by the present owner. It is remarkable for the immense twin herbaceous borders, backed by clipped yew hedges and separated by a wide grass walk, which lead from the formal, stone-balustraded terraces around the house to the River Ure, where they are terminated by similar balustrading flanking stone steps leading down to a landing stage. This walk is centred on the south front of the house and is crossed by another narrower avenue, also yew enclosed and with numerous statues. The two provide the formal framework around which a number of smaller gardens have been created. One is a rose garden planted mainly with old-fashioned varieties and species. Another is an iris and peony garden; a third, known as Sylvia's Garden, is sunken and paved and planted mainly with compact trailing plants. There is a garden devoted mainly to flowers of late summer and autumn and others planted respectively with red and yellow flowers, blue and white flowers, and yet a third to give a grey and purple effect. A great many fine trees and shrubs have been planted, many of uncommon kinds and some which might have been expected to be too tender for the locality, but have nevertheless thrived. A rock and water garden of considerable size is situated near the river, but is now mainly planted with shrubs.

The twin herbaceous borders leading to Newby Hall

Parcevall Hall

Appletreewick, Yorkshire. One mile north-east of Appletreewick off the B6265 from Pateley Bridge to Skipton. Privately owned. Open on Tuesdays and Wednesdays from May to September.

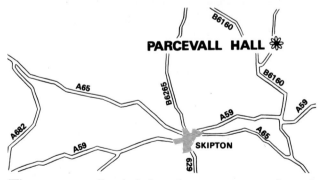

Parcevall Hall is a long, low, grey building standing in a fold of the Yorkshire moors. It is itself at an elevation of about 600 feet and it faces Simon Seat, one of the highest points in this part of Yorkshire. Someone once said that from a distance it looked like a Tibetan monastery, an apt description of the bleakness and remoteness of the scene. Yet in this unpromising spot a fascinating garden has been made.

Below the house the land is terraced, but elsewhere the garden follows the natural contours of the hill. There is even a great outcrop of rock in the entrance court which has been planted with imagination. Behind this is a more formally-constructed rock and water garden leading, surprisingly, to an apple orchard from which there are fine views of the valley of the River Wharfe.

There are woodlands below the terraces, cut through by a little torrent which at one point has been made to fill a deep pool. In this wood, and another at a little distance, there are many rhododendrons, including a fine collection of Chinese species. The terraces themselves are stocked with good plants, some surprisingly tender for so cold and exposed a situation. There are even borders crammed with the pink South African *Nerine bowdenii,* a lovely member of the amaryllis family which flowers freely here.

Left. The water-lily pool at Parcevall Hall

Above. Two scenes at Castle Howard. The Temple of the Four Winds placed at the summit of the long walk from the house with the Mausoleum on a more distant ridge, and below, the Roman bridge across the river-like lake in the valley below these buildings

Castle Howard

Coneysthorpe, Yorkshire. Five miles west of Malton on the road from the A64, at Barton Hill to Slingsby. Privately owned. Open daily, except on Mondays and Fridays, from early April to early October, also open on Bank Holiday Mondays.

Castle Howard was the first palatial mansion designed by Vanbrugh, work starting on it in 1702, three years earlier than on his second great commission, Blenheim Palace (see p. 79). As at Blenheim, an elaborate formal garden was planned for it, but Castle Howard did not have to wait half a century for the arrival of Lancelot Brown to give it a landscape garden as well. For the 3rd Earl of Carlisle was himself keenly interested in the new ideas about more natural methods of garden making which were then being discussed, and, with the help of Vanbrugh and the architect Hawksmoor, he began to put them into effect on the grand scale at Castle Howard. Some of what he created has disappeared but much remains.

The house stands on a ridge which continues beyond it in a semi-circle with several little eminences facing south. These have been given greater significance by placing buildings on them, a particularly beautiful pavilion, the Temple of the Four Winds, nearest to the house and, further away, a big domed mausoleum.

In the valley below are lakes, one large and broad, another, crossed by a stone bridge, long, narrow and river-like. Other objects are placed as eye-catchers in the distance, including a large pyramid. Originally there were many statues but a lot of these have now disappeared. So has the original parterre in front of the house, but it has been replaced by another designed by W. A. Nesfield in 1850. It is suitably impressive, with a baroque fountain, representing Tritons supporting a globe, as a central feature, and clipped hedges of yew to give it substance and pattern. A large walled garden beside the parterre has some remarkable gates.

The road by which Castle Howard is approached is itself an avenue passing up and over the ridge at a little distance from the house to which it is linked by a cross avenue. Where they meet is an obelisk. The road passes through two elaborate archways, and there is a bastioned wall for good measure.

In the valley to the north is another even larger lake, but on this side there are no architectural objects and the landscape is simpler. Throughout trees are used to heighten the scenic and dramatic effects of this early essay in landscape gardening.

Ness

Neston, Cheshire. At Neston on the B5135 off the A540 from Chester to Hoylake. University of Liverpool. Open daily throughout the year except for Christmas Day.

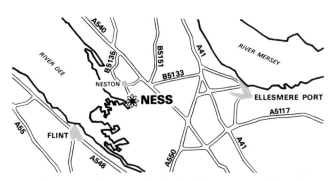

This garden, on the exposed Wirral peninsula, was made by the late A. K. Bulley at the beginning of this century, and from its earliest days was opened to the public with the intention of increasing interest in hardy plants. Mr Bulley contributed generously to plant hunting expeditions and himself sent George Forrest to Asia in search of primulas, meconopses and other plants in which he was interested. After his death the garden was neglected for a period until it was handed over to the University of Liverpool for scientific work, but with the stipulation that it should still be open to the public as Mr Bulley would have wished.

Though some of the original planting remains, including a wonderful drift of snowflakes (leucojum), the garden itself has been largely remodelled by the university authorities. The house, which occupies a central position on a knoll, is used as offices and behind it, on the rocky slopes facing the Dee estuary, one of the finest heather gardens in the country has been made. To the south there is a dell in which Mr Bulley made his original rock beds, and which now contains a more conventional rock garden with stream and pool. It is reached by way of a small, neatly-made terrace garden.

To the north a great sweep of lawn is bordered by an immensely long shrub border leading to a smaller area planned in the now popular island bed manner. There is a good rose garden, herbaceous borders and other features of interest to garden makers and planners. Despite its old associations, this is in many ways a young garden reflecting the taste of the day which gives it an added importance.

Valley Garden

Harrogate, Yorkshire. In Harrogate. The Harrogate Urban District Council. Open daily all the year round.

Were it not for additions made since about 1930, the Valley Garden would simply rank as an attractive public park, particularly well sited in a valley which extends into the centre of Harrogate, and with the added attraction of a stream running through it. But in recent years so much planting has been carried out of plants normally considered rare or difficult, that the Valley Garden draws interested gardeners from all parts of the world. A fine peat garden has been constructed for the cultivation of meconopses, lime-hating primulas and other plants, and a very long and beautiful rock garden has been made to follow the stream. On higher ground at the head of the valley a great many rhododendrons have been naturalised in native woodland and, here again, meconopses of many kinds thrive.

Opposite top left. The rock garden dell at Ness

Opposite bottom. The splendidly-planted and very fine heather bank at Ness

Opposite top right. A selection of rock plants in the Valley Garden, Harrogate

Right. Streamside planting in the Valley Garden

Below. The new glade garden at Rudding Park

Rudding Park

Harrogate, Yorkshire. One mile south-east of Harrogate off the A661 to Wetherby. Privately owned. Open daily, except Fridays, from Easter to October.

Rudding Park is a Regency house, well placed on high ground with parkland to the south and east. The garden is mainly to the west and is in two sections: first a series of avenues radiate through woodland from a large grass circle with a big marble vase in the centre, and then, further west down one of these avenues, a rose garden and a walled kitchen garden are situated.

No doubt originally the woodland garden contained little in the way of plants beyond the trees and under-growth necessary to produce the dark, chancel effect of avenues of this kind, but later generations have added many flowering shrubs and ornamental plants and this work of diversification is continuing to the present day. Indeed, in the northern part of the wood, what is virtually a new garden is growing up in the popular island bed or glade style, and a stream which runs through this part has been heavily planted with moisture-loving primulas and good foliage plants. There are many fine hybrid rhododendrons and azaleas throughout the wood, beside the entrance drive and around a chapel that stands next to the house, and also good plantations of hydrangeas for a summer display.

The rose garden is semi-formal in character and contains many old-fashioned hybrid musk, vigorous floribunda, and shrub varieties which have grown into very large bushes. Round about there are other shrubs, including mock oranges (philadelphus) to scent the air in summer, and mahonias for winter and spring flower and fragrance.

The avenue continues through the rose garden to a wrought-iron gate in the wall of the kitchen garden, through which a straight path leads between double herbaceous borders, backed by yew hedges, to a little brick pavilion in the style of an orangery. Around the house there are lawns on which peacocks strut and some fine old trees and, in an angle of the building, beneath the library windows, a little formal herb garden.

Chatsworth

Edensor, Derbyshire. Three miles east of Bakewell on the A623 between Little Rowsley and Sparrowpit. Privately owned. Open daily from early April to early October.

Garden making has been an almost continuous process at Chatsworth for 300 years and is not yet completed, so that within itself it contains a history of garden styles. Here may be seen intact the Great Cascade designed for the 1st Duke of Devonshire in the latter half of the 17th century by Grillet, a pupil of Le Nôtre. Here, too, is the Canal Pond, a long formal stretch of water reflecting the south face of the mansion and the beautiful Seahorse Fountain designed by Cibber, the multiple jets of which are fed by water from the Great Cascade.

The famous 17th-century gardeners George London and Henry Wise worked at Chatsworth, but their formal parterres were later swept away by Lancelot Brown who landscaped some parts of the garden and surrounding park in the manner of the 18th century. However, two delightful buildings remain from the earlier period, Flora's Temple, originally a garden house for a bowling green but now moved to a new position at the termination of the Broad Walk, and a greenhouse in front of which an enclosed rose garden has been made.

Joseph Paxton was engaged as head gardener in 1826 by the 6th Duke of Devonshire, and in the ensuing years many more changes were made at Chatsworth. Most famous was the building of the Great Conservatory, precursor of the Crystal Palace which was to house the Great Exhibition in 1851. This conservatory had to be removed after the First World War, and its place is taken by a series of enclosed gardens and a maze which is still in the early stages of formation. But many of Paxton's other additions remain, notably the Emperor Fountain at the north end of the Canal Pond, which can throw a jet of water nearly 300 feet into the air; the strange Willow Tree Fountain made of metal in the form of a tree and spurting water from its hollow branches, and the extensive natural rock and water gardens.

It was during this period, too, that most of the trees and shrubs, which to day contribute so largely to the beauty of Chatsworth, were planted. An extensive arboretum was established on the hillside behind the house, and to the south a pinetum was made to contain many species newly introduced from America. Planting of trees and shrubs continues, and some new formal features have been added in recent years, including a serpentine walk between beech hedges, linking an earlier formal feature, the Ring Pond, with a bust of the 6th Duke of Devonshire on a column at a higher level; and the pleached limes which flank the lawns to the south of the house and so pleasantly continue the formal lines of the Canal Pond.

Opposite left. Fountains and Canal Pond at Chatsworth

Below. View of the Cascade, Chatsworth

Fountains Abbey

Fountains Abbey from the River Skell

Three miles south-west of Ripon off the B6265 from Ripon to Pateley Bridge. The Ministry of Public Building and Works. Open daily throughout the year.

The names of Fountains Abbey and Studley Royal are now inseparable for the gardener. They began, however, as entirely separate entities, the Abbey as a Cistercian monastery placed in a valley and built in part over the stream which flowed through it; Studley Park as the grounds surrounding the nearby home of John Aislabie, Chancellor in Walpole's government. The two sites were eventually united by John Aislabie's son, who, about 1760, purchased the ruined abbey and used it to complete a scheme conceived by his father. This combined work illustrates the transition between the formal style of the 17th century and the landscape gardening of the 18th century.

Water enters very largely into the design and is obtained entirely from the River Skell which flows into the more open grounds of Studley Park from the comparatively closed-in valley of the monastery. In the lower part of this valley, out of sight of the Abbey, the scheme is formal, consisting of a long canal, flanked on one side by a huge circular pool and two crescent pools, and on the other by a smaller U-shaped pool. The canal is terminated by a stone balustrade and two stone pavilions between which the water cascades into a lake in Studley Park.

These formal waterworks are overlooked by a temple

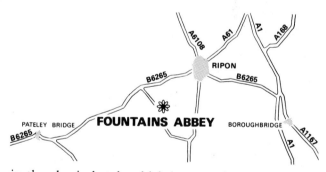

in the classical style which is centred on the circular pool. This is known as the Moon Pool, possibly from its shape or because John Aislabie, so it is said, planned this garden to be seen by moonlight. The whole area, backed by the heavily-wooded slopes of the valley, he named the Arena of the Great Amphitheatre, which aptly describes its character and extent.

His son, in extending the gardens to the abbey, adopted a much more informal approach. First he created a fine lake, roughly in the shape of a horseshoe, but without the rigid outline of the pools below, and then a great stretch of grass bordered by the River Skell which was widened and more sharply defined to give added point to the composition, the whole held within the heavily-wooded slopes of the valley. This simple treatment focuses attention on the ruined Gothic Abbey which terminates the landscape in a highly dramatic manner.

The Northern Hills

reach the eastern edge of the Cumbrian Mountains at Penrith. From here it is only a short distance to the Lakes of Westmorland and Cumberland and if he continues northwards he will cross the Solway Plain to enter Scotland just north of Carlisle.

This is the area that I have chosen to lump together as the Northern Hills, for though some of it is in England and some in Scotland, it is climate and topography rather than nationality that have determined the character of its gardens. Moreover from the standpoint of the tourist it is a reasonable unit, well served by radiating roads and, therefore, quite easily covered from two or three starting points.

As might be expected from the character of the country the finest gardens here are mostly wild or woodland. At Muncaster Castle in Cumberland the magnificent scenery of Eskdale has been exploited to the full, also the mild, moist climate which has made it possible to grow one of the finest and largest rhododendrons collections in England. To the east, at Howick Hall, a woodland garden demonstrates that even the North Sea can have an ameliorating effect on the climate, enabling surprisingly tender plants to be grown, while in the centre, at Dawyck, is proof that the coldest climate need not prevent the formation of a great garden. There are many more spectacular gardens in the area: White Craggs at the north end of Lake Windermere, Cragside Grounds in Rothbury Forest on the northern edge of the Cheviots, and The Hirsel just north of the Tweed at Coldstream, and in nearly all of them it is rhododendrons and azaleas that provide a great part of the spectacle not already supplied by the site itself.

A traveller to the north from Yorkshire can follow several alternative routes but each will take him over, or by, considerable ranges of hills. If he chooses the Great North Road, now the A1, he will keep most closely to the wide Vale of York and the coastal strip. Passing the Yorkshire Moors on his right, he will have the long line of the Pennine Chain to his left, and as he approaches the Border and enters Scotland he will skirt first the Cheviot Hills, then the Lammermuir Hills and finally, before entering Edinburgh, the Pentland Hills. Should he choose to branch off above Morpeth on to the A697 or at Newcastle on to the A696, he will find himself more deeply involved with these Northern Hills and crossing some very beautiful country; while if he strikes north-westwards from Scotch Corner, south of Darlington, he will cross the Pennines to

Cragside perched on its wild Northumbrian hillside

Cragside Grounds

Rothbury, Northumberland. Half-a-mile east of Rothbury on the B6341 to Alnwick. Privately owned. Open daily from Easter to September.

This is not so much a garden as a scenic drive, several miles long, through wildly-beautiful Northumbrian hillside and valley in which there are several large lakes, numerous outcrops of rock, some immense, and many trees. In the lusher parts it is planted as woodland, and on the dry and exposed hillsides it has a sparse covering of pine and spruce with almost everywhere a dense undergrowth of rhododendrons and azaleas. These are mainly the common purple and yellow kinds giving a peak display in June, when this strange garden is at its most beautiful. The house is perched on a shelf on the side of a steep and craggy hill with a stream in the valley below, and here there is an area of more sophisticated planting with hybrid rhododendrons and other shrubs.

Levens Hall

Levens, Westmorland. Five miles south of Kendal on the A6 to Lancaster. Privately owned. Open daily from May to mid-September.

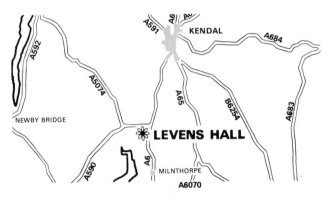

The topiary garden at Levens is one of the oldest and best preserved in the country. It is usually attributed to a French gardener named Beaumont, who was gardener to James II and had been a pupil of Le Nôtre, but it seems possible that the main topiary garden, with its rather crowded specimens in a variety of fantastic shapes, is even earlier than this and a relic of Jacobean times. Some of the specimens are of box, some of yew, and there is a pleasing contrast between green and golden varieties, which adds considerably to the charm of the garden.

To one side of this topiary garden is an excellent rose garden, and to the other is a formally-designed garden in which clipped beech encloses a large circle of grass from which alleyways radiate at right angles. Beyond the confines of the garden proper, the east-west alley is continued into the surrounding country as tree avenues. The one to the west starts on the far side of the main A6 road (which here skirts the garden wall), and shortly turns to run roughly parallel with the River Kent until it overlooks it about a mile to the north-east. The visitor following this route can return by a path beside the river. It is these large-scale formal features that can be attributed with more certainty to Beaumont.

Opposite. The elaborate topiary garden at Levens Hall, made towards the end of the 17th century and above two of the many elaborately-patterned topiary specimens at Levens Hall cut in yew or box

Above. This elegant stone basin, fountain and pool surrounded by rhododendrons is one of the many features occurring unexpectedly throughout the garden at Holker Hall

Holker Hall

Cark in Cartmel, Lancashire. Three-and-a-half miles west of Grange over Sands on the B5278 from Cark in Cartmel to Haverthwaite. Privately owned. Open daily, except Fridays, from Easter Saturday to early October.

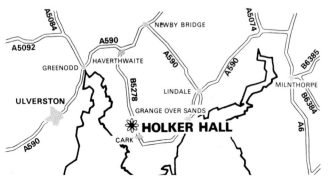

The extensive garden at Holker Hall combines many features in a somewhat unusual way. Much of it is laid out in the parkland manner fashionable in the 19th century, with many fine trees and shrubs spaced out as specimens in grass in which daffodils, bluebells and other bulbs were once planted and have subsequently naturalised.

There are, however, numerous more formal features, which are not kept, as is so commonly the case in such gardens, to the area around the house, but appear as surprises at various points in the grounds. In one glade of rhododendrons a fountain plays into a fine stone basin raised on a pedestal. A flight of stone steps leads to an avenue of weeping cherries, and at some distance from the house the visitor comes suddenly upon a formal rose garden.

Elsewhere in the garden there are also large belts of rhododendrons, mainly the hardy hybrid varieties, which make a great display in late spring and early summer. Around the house are terraces laid out as parterres, and planted with roses.

The Hirsel

(Dundock Wood), Coldstream, Berwickshire. Two miles west of Coldstream on the A697 to Greenlaw. Privately owned. Open daily throughout the year.

A fine example of woodland gardening in which mixed broad-leaf and conifer woodland (including a tulip tree said to be over 200 years old) has been heavily underplanted with rhododendrons and azaleas. Grass avenues and winding paths provide some long vistas and numerous viewpoints. The woodland is pleasant at all seasons, but blazes into full colour in late May and, more or less, throughout June, since the underplanting is mainly with the yellow azalea and with late-flowering hardy hybrid rhododendrons in which hybrids of *Rhododendron ponticum* predominate. The azaleas also give good autumn colour. Dundock Wood is of some historic interest as being one of the first woodland gardens of its kind in Scotland, planting of *Rhododendron ponticum* and hardy hybrid rhododendrons having started there in the mid-19th century.

Muncaster Castle

Ravenglass, Cumberland. One mile east of Ravenglass on the A595 to Bootle. Privately owned. Open every Sunday and occasionally on other days for charity.

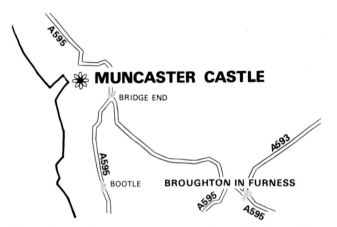

The castle, built of a warm red stone, dates from the 13th century, but there have been many additions and alterations since. It stands in a position of great natural beauty on a low hill at the foot of Eskdale, with views up the valley to the 3000-foot heights of Scafell and Bow Fell. The oldest part of the garden is a grass terrace, half-a-mile in length, which sweeps around the hillside following the 100-foot contour and providing a panoramic view of this remarkable scenery. It was made about 1780 when landscaping was in vogue, and probably some of the adjoining woodlands and tree belts were planted about the same period. The terrace is essentially a formal feature, made for promenading, and its formality is intensified by the low parapet-like hedge of box and yew by which it is bounded, the box trimmed to a round top, the yew flat topped and a little taller.

Into this lovely setting 19th- and 20th-century planters have introduced one of the finest collections in the north of England of rhododendrons, azaleas and other trees and shrubs. Many of these are massed in a steep valley, the Ghyll, which separates the terrace from the castle; many more are planted in the rather dense woodland and more open glades which flank the long drive leading from the main road to the castle. Here will be found some of the largest specimen rhododendrons, growing with jungle-like profusion, thanks to the mild climate and heavy rainfall, and interspersed with large groups of bamboos. In the Ghyll many Japanese acers and hydrangeas have been planted to increase and extend the colour effect. To the west of the castle there is a more formal enclosed garden, a large lawn and beds once filled with flowers in season but now permanently planted with shrubs including many evergreen azaleas.

White Craggs

Clappersgate, Westmorland. One mile southwest of Ambleside on the A593 to Coniston. Privately owned. Open daily throughout the year.

A notable example of a rock garden which, because of the nature of the site on a steep hillside at the head of Lake Windermere, required only a minimum of shaping and rearranging to convert it from the wild into a garden. The planting is mainly with shrubs rather than with rock plants, though some of the more vigorous kinds, as well as small herbaceous plants, are used to extend the flowering season and furnish the more open places. But, in general, it is great masses of evergreen and deciduous azaleas and rhododendrons that fill this garden with colour and make late spring its peak season. However, it is beautiful at all times of the year because of the scenic qualities of the site, which include fine views of Lake Windermere.

Opposite top. Rhododendrons and azaleas in Dundock Wood, The Hirsel, an early woodland planting

Opposite bottom. The ghyll at Muncaster Castle filled with rhododendrons, azaleas, maples and other shrubs

Sizergh Castle

Kendal, Westmorland. Three-and-a-half miles south of Kendal on the A6 to Lancaster. The National Trust. Open on Tuesdays, Wednesdays and Thursdays from April to September.

Interest at Sizergh Castle must inevitably centre on the house, some parts of which are of great age and all of which is beautiful. The garden is ancillary to this, but it is well worthy of inspection as it contains an exceptionally fine example of 'natural' rock gardening with local weather-worn Westmorland stone. This is in the form of a shallow bowl with a little pool in the middle, the whole ringed with trees and shrubs. The rock work was made early in the present century, by Mr Hayes of Kendal, a professional garden designer specialising in rock gardens, and this is one of the most notable examples of his work. As with so many gardens of this kind, the planting is with small herbaceous plants rather than with genuine alpines, but there is also a noteworthy collection of hardy ferns containing many beautiful forms of native species.

Beyond the rock garden is a much larger, more formal pool, or small lake, below a series of formal terraces, and here again there is interest in the way in which the long flights of stone steps leading down from the house have been gradually widened to change the perspective. A recent addition to one of the terraces is a double avenue of pleached limes.

The lake and terraces at Sizergh Castle

The rock garden and pool at Sizergh Castle

Howick Hall

Howick, Northumberland. Five miles north-east of Alnwick on the B1339 from Lesbury to Embleton. Privately owned. Open daily from mid-April to the end of August.

The fine Georgian mansion of warm yellow stone, built in 1776, is situated about a mile from the North Sea from which it is protected by a low ridge and woodland. The land falls away on the south side to Howick Burn and has been terraced in front of the house, each terrace being treated differently: one with raised beds for alpine plants, another planted with roses and lavender, a third mainly with irises, a fourth containing a fountain and pool.

Hardy African lilies (agapanthus) grow almost wild on these sunny terraces, and the sheltered walls of the house have been used to protect a number of rather tender plants and shrubs, some now grown to great size. Throughout, the planting is of great interest and beauty. A path and bridge lead to the church on the far side of the brook, but only the belfry is visible from the terraces, the rest being screened by the large beeches, oaks, holm oaks and cedars which hem the garden in on almost every side, some dating back to the

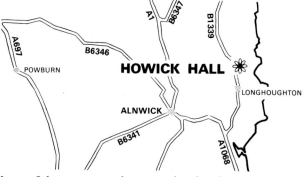

late 18th century when much planting was carried out.

But the greatest interest to-day lies in Silver Wood, a woodland garden made since 1890 and now fully matured. It lies a little to the east and is reached by a walk through an informal area of grass and shrubs underplanted with meadow saffrons, daffodils and other bulbs. The wood itself is of Scots pine and hardwoods with some good blue cedars, and it is heavily underplanted with the finest rhododendrons, azaleas, magnolias, hydrangeas, meconopses, primulas, peonies, heathers and many other delightful plants. It is an excellent example of the kind of wild gardening which, after a time, becomes almost self-maintaining and requires a minimum of attention.

Dawyck House

Stobo, Peeblesshire. Seven miles south-west of Peebles on the B712 from Peebles to Rachan Mill. Privately owned. Open on Wednesdays, Saturdays and Sundays from late April to August.

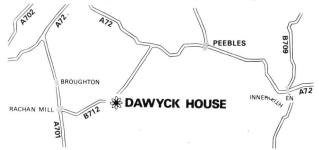

Originally planned for the trial of forest trees with a view to their use in commercial forestry (the European larch was first grown at Dawyck in 1725), the garden has been greatly enriched by the introduction of many ornamental trees and shrubs including a particularly fine collection of rhododendrons.

The site, in the valley of the River Tweed, is exceptionally beautiful. Conifer forest covers much of the hillside to the south, but a wide ride cut through it allows an uninterrupted view from the house. Around the house the treatment is simple and formal with grass terraces surrounded with stone balustrades ornamented with stone urns and balls. Though the rest of the garden is woodland and meadow, similar architectural features recur throughout, giving an element of sophistication unusual in a garden of this type. A burn tumbles down the hillside and is crossed by an attractive hump-backed bridge of more rustic character and known as the Dutch Bridge. But, for all its attractive and varied architectural features, it is for its marvellous collection of trees and shrubs that Dawyck will be principally admired. There are splendid conifers of all kinds and a great many broad-leaved trees. The fastigiate beech originated here and is known as the Dawyck beech. There is an unusually narrow, columnar form of oak, fine specimens of Brewer's spruce and a great many rhododendrons, including some which are seldom seen in such good health in British gardens.

In spring the meadows near the house are filled with a profusion of daffodils, and the skunk cabbage (lysichitum) unfolds its huge yellow or white spathes beside the stream. Dawyck is of particular interest since it is situated in a very cold part of Scotland where, nevertheless, a great variety of exotic plants seem to thrive exceedingly well.

Above. Wild gardening in Silver Wood at Howick Hall

Below. Rhododendron souliei in the Dawyck woodland

Below right. Ornamental steps at Dawyck

Mellerstain

Gordon, Berwickshire. Six miles north-west of Kelso off the A6089 to Gordon. Privately owned. Open daily, except Saturdays, from May to September.

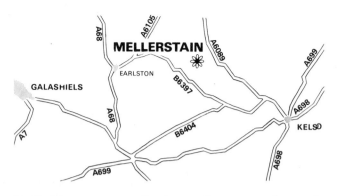

Mellerstain is a magnificent 18th-century mansion, partly to the design of William Adam, but finished later in the century by his son, Robert Adam. So perfectly does its garden fit it, that it is with astonishment one discovers not only that it is not contemporary, but also that in its present form it has only been in existence since 1909. It was planned by Sir Reginald Blomfield and consists of elaborate terraces linked by a long grass slope with a large lake at the foot enclosed by trees. An unusual element of formality is given to this grass slope by enclosing it within hedges which converge in a waisted curve towards the lake. The upper terrace laps around the lower and is linked with it by curving stairways. Terraces and stairways are handsomely balustraded and ornamented with urns and stone vases, and the upper terrace is planted as a rose garden with beds, mainly for hybrid tea varieties, and with climbing roses on the house. More flower borders flank the terraces, and there is a great deal of open park planting with specimen trees and shrubs.

Daffodils are naturalised on the grass slopes to increase the spring display; there are rhododendrons and azaleas for May and June and good flower borders and hydrangeas to maintain colour into late summer.

For those interested in the history of garden design it is worthy of note that the present very natural-looking lake was developed from a formal canal-like stretch of water that formed part of the original 18th-century garden which has now completely disappeared.

Mellerstain with its terraces and patterned grass slope viewed from the end of the great lake

Wallington

The stream which flows through the walled garden at Wallington, with the terrace on the right

Cambo, Northumberland. One mile south of Cambo on B6342 just north of its junction with A696. The National Trust. Open daily from April to September.

The visitor's first sight of the gardens of Wallington is of a row of large stone gargoyles standing on the lawn and grinning at him across the ha-ha – an intimation that this is an unusual garden. Yet the early stages of exploration do not reveal anything else of great note. There is a simple and dignified Georgian house approached through a large courtyard ringed by domestic buildings and cottages of the same period; a large lawn flanked by well-stocked flower borders and with some good specimen trees and groups of golden yew – and those grinning gargoyles.

In fact the main garden is some distance away across the road, through a wood and past a lake. It is a walled garden which looks as if it may originally have been intended for fruit and vegetables, but now it is entirely ornamental. It occupies a small, curving valley through which a stream runs. One side and the upper end of the valley have been terraced and there is a large conservatory backed by a brick pavilion. On the parapet of the long terrace are a number of enchanting little lead figures – not just conventional shepherds and shepherdesses, but milkmaids, aphrodites, courtiers, Roman soldiers and other more enigmatic figures. The conservatory contains some of the oldest, largest and finest fuchsias to be seen anywhere in the country.

The rest of the garden follows the two-way contour of the valley. Much of it is lawn through which a stream trickles between rocks nearly concealed by small-flowering plants. Ornamental trees are planted as if they were forming a small orchard, each surrounded by a neat circle of cultivated ground entirely covered in one kind of flower, violas in one, stonecrops in another and so on. The whole of the bottom of the valley is given up to flowers, in what are virtually nursery beds, and one reads without surprise that this is the garden of a keen flower arranger. The effect is completely delightful.

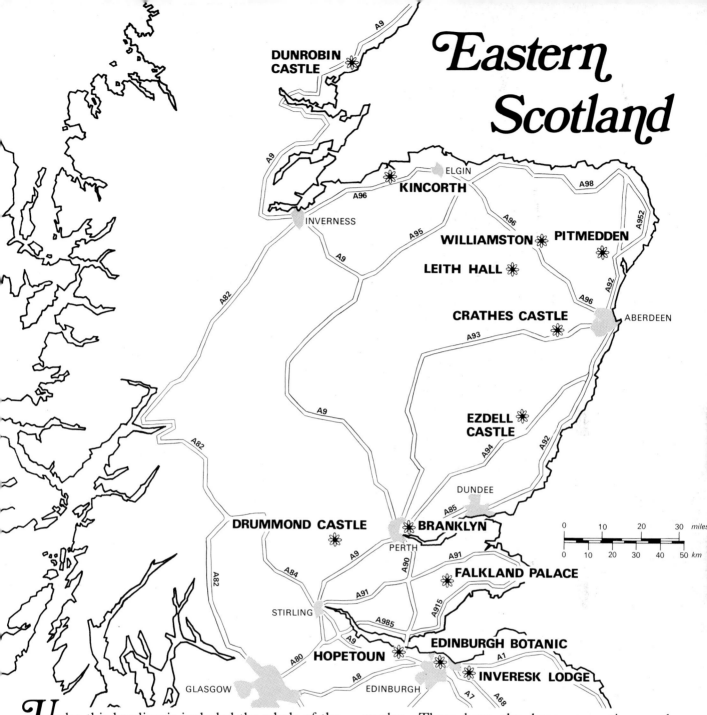

Under this heading is included the whole of the eastern half of Scotland north of Edinburgh. Where the Grampian Mountains cut through it the climate is too harsh and the soil too poor to permit much gardening, but all along the coastal belt are fine estates and romantic castles some with the loveliest and most surprising gardens. At Edzell is a delightful ruin in which the exquisitely carved wall of a Renaissance garden has been miraculously preserved. It has been given a suitably elaborate knot garden to match and is a delight that no connoisseur of old gardens should miss. Pitmedden is of similar date and far greater size, and at Crathes Castle clever modern additions and superb planting have greatly increased the interest of another very old

garden. There have also been renovations and additions to the gardens of Falkland Palace, and at Drummond Castle a 10-acre parterre originally laid out in the 17th century is still splendidly maintained.

But, lest anyone thinks from this brief catalogue that the gardens of Eastern Scotland are predominantly formal, there is Edinburgh Botanic Garden, filled with good plants, and skilfully landscaped to provide some of the most beautiful views of the city of Edinburgh. The new plant houses there are a triumph of modern horticultural building and contain fine selections of plants arranged with great skill.

Finally there are a number of attractive small gardens of which one, Branklyn at Perth, is considered by many experts to be the most perfect example of a miniaturised 'natural' garden in the British Isles.

The pond in the Edinburgh Botanic Garden

Dunrobin Castle

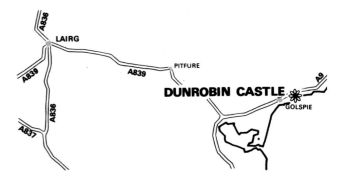

**Golspie, Sutherland. At Golspie, twenty miles
north-east of Bonar Bridge on the A9 to Helms-
dale. Privately owned. Open daily, except Sundays, from mid-July to mid-September.**

The house is an exuberant example of the Scottish
baronial style, perched on the edge of an escarpment
looking south over the North Sea, which is only a few
hundred yards away. Elegant stone-balustraded terraces and stairways were designed for this steep slope
by Sir Charles Barry in the mid-19th century, and
these provide vantage points for viewing the elaborate
parterres which have been laid out on the level ground
below.

The situation and treatment invite comparison with
Drummond Castle in Perthshire, but here there is the
sea, instead of wooded countryside for background,
and the whole is smaller and more intimate in conception. There are three separate parterres, each with
its pool and fountain as a central feature and with beds
lined with box. More cones and mop-heads of box
accent the design, and against the great balustraded
wall of one parterre is a long border itself divided into
compartments with box to match the whole scheme.
Each parterre has its own design, one circular, two
rectangular and they are separated one from another
by dense belts of shrubs so that, though all can be
viewed from above, at ground level each appears
separately. To-day the parterres are planted with free-
flowering floribunda roses and the long border
beneath the terrace wall mainly with perennial plants.
No doubt in Victorian times all were filled with
bedding plants in season, but cost of upkeep has
necessitated the change to less labour-consuming
planting. It is highly effective.

Drummond Castle

Crieff, Perthshire. One mile south of Crieff on the A822 road to Dunblane. Privately owned. Open on Saturdays and Wednesdays from April to mid-August.

The rather stark grey stone castle dating from the late 15th century and the long, low mansion in Scottish baronial style which flanks it, stand on a high ridge of land overlooking a valley to the south. The site, with its sudden change in levels, is reminiscent of Powis Castle (see p. 95), but at Drummond Castle the main garden is not on the stone terraces which sustain the slope, but in the valley, the terraces serving mainly as viewpoints from which the great formal pattern below can be admired.

The effect is all the more dramatic because the visitor comes upon it suddenly, emerging from the bare courtyard of the castle on to the uppermost terrace. The parterre is laid out roughly in the form of a St Andrew's Cross. Beyond it are woodlands through which a wide avenue has been left so that the eye is directed far away into the landscape, a fitting contrast to the intricate formality of the foreground. An elaborate stone staircase, in scale with the whole design, descends the slope centrally, dividing and rejoining as it goes, and adorned with numerous statues and ornaments. On each side, the bank is planted with heathers and other low-growing shrubs in a kind of tartan pattern.

The parterre is terminated to the east by a stone bridge, beneath and beyond which is an informal lake blending into parkland. Stone buildings in classical style and a variety of statues decorate the parterre which is further diversified and made more three-dimensional by clipped evergreens, some in the form of columns, some shaped like enormous toadstools. A central feature is an extraordinary multiplex sundial bearing the date 1630.

The original parterre at Drummond Castle was laid out in the mid-17th century but the elaborate ornamentation was not added until 200 years later. The whole has been restored and the planting simplified in recent years. Some of the patterned beds are filled with flowers in season to accentuate and enliven the design and it is in high summer that this garden can be seen at its most colourful, though the profusion of architectural features, the evergreen shrubs and trees and the general firmness of design ensure that it will captivate the eye at all times of the year.

Opposite. One of the parterres at Dunrobin Castle

Below. The great 10-acre parterre at Drummond Castle planned as a St Andrew's Cross

Hopetoun House

South Queensferry, West Lothian. Two miles west of South Queensferry off the A904 to Bo'ness. Privately owned. Open daily, except Thursdays and Fridays, from May to September.

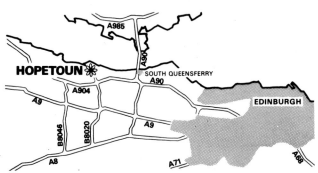

One of the few examples in Scotland of 18th-century landscape, the garden to the south of the house is semi-formal in character with a large circular pool in a sunken lawn as a feature in the middle distance. This is backed by a semi-circle of radiating rides rough cut through the woodland. To the north, facing the Firth of Forth, is a much more formal design with a huge area of lawn encircled by the drive, intersected by gravelled walks and guarded by sphinxes. The railway and the road bridges over the Firth of Forth can be seen, but not the water of the Firth, and it is interesting to observe that though from the west end of the house there are magnificent views up the Firth towards Culross, no use has been made of these by the 18th-century garden designer, who appears rather to have set out to exclude them from his landscape.

At some distance from the main garden, beside the walled kitchen garden, is an attractive modern rose garden simply laid out with long rectangular beds filled with modern floribunda varieties, together with a central circular pool and stone fountain.

Above. Aerial view of the garden of Hopetoun House

Below. The Renaissance garden of Edzell Castle

Edzell Castle

Edzell, Angus. One mile north of Edzell on the B966 to Fettercairn. The Ministry of Public Building and Works. Open daily throughout the year.

Edzell Castle was built and extended during the 16th century as much as a dignified and beautiful mansion to be lived in as a fortress to be defended. It is now a ruin of considerable interest to antiquaries, as is the walled garden on the south side, which is the main attraction for garden lovers. This is a unique example of the Renaissance influence on the art of garden making and it has been beautifully restored and maintained by the Ministry of Public Building and Works.

The high wall, built of the same deep rose-coloured sandstone as the castle, is unusually elaborate in design with numerous recesses, some quite small and arranged in a chequered pattern, others larger and placed singly, and all meant to accommodate plants. There are also carved panels depicting the Planetary Dieties, the Liberal Arts and the Cardinal Virtues, and on the coping, arched and carved niches, now empty but presumably intended for the display of busts. The walls are hollow, with circular holes pierced through the centres of carved stars just below the coping to permit birds to enter and nest therein. Originally the recesses were painted and planted in blue and white which, with the reddish colour of the sandstone, represented the heraldic colours of the Edzell Lindsays who owned the property. To-day they are not painted but simply planted with lobelia and alyssum.

At one corner is a garden house of matching construction, and the large rectangle enclosed by the wall is a parterre or knot garden with the quite elaborate designs defined by closely-trimmed box and displayed on a ground work of close-mown turf. The whole effect is completely delightful.

Pitmedden

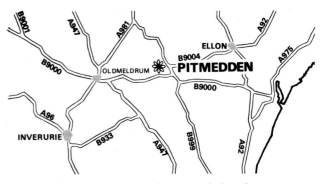

Pitmedden, Aberdeenshire. Five miles east of Oldmeldrum on B999, from A92 (north of Aberdeen), to Tarves. The National Trust for Scotland. Open daily throughout the year.

As at Edzell Castle, the framework of a Renaissance garden has been used for a wonderfully effective 20th-century reconstruction in the style of the original, but with flowers many of which would not have been available when the garden was originally laid out by Sir Alexander Seton in 1675. Both gardens are rectangular, entirely geometric in design, and enclosed by walls, and in both elaborate patterns, including mottoes and inscriptions, are carried out in living material, either clipped box or flowers. But there resemblance ends, for whereas the garden at Edzell Castle is small and intimate and the walls elaborately fashioned and carved, the Great Garden at Pitmedden justifies its name by being 3 acres in extent, and the walls are of rough dressed stone with little ornament.

Moreover, the gardens at Pitmedden are fashioned on naturally sloping ground from which the Great Garden has been scooped out, and the upper garden built up into a high level terrace from which to look down on the richly-patterned parterres below. Twin flights of stone steps flanked by tall stone pillars lead from this upper terrace to the parterres, and at each end of the terrace is a large and handsome stone pavilion standing in the angle of the wall.

There are four rectangular parterres each with its own distinctive design, and in the centre there is a large stone fountain constructed partly from the Cross Fountain of Linlithgow and partly of pieces from an original Pitmedden fountain of the same period. The ends of the Great Garden are also enclosed by terrace walls, and a high wall on the fourth side completes the enclosure.

The upper garden is mainly lawn with only a modest amount of planting and ornament and, at present, serves mainly as a viewing platform for the Great Garden below, though there are plans for further development, when funds permit, possibly including a garden of herbs and medicinal plants.

The Great Garden of Pitmedden House

Crathes Castle

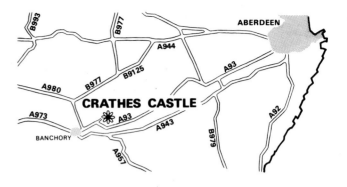

Banchory, Kincardineshire. Two miles east of Banchory on the A93 to Aberdeen. The National Trust for Scotland. Open daily throughout the year.

This very romantic-looking castle was built during the latter half of the 16th century and garden making on the steep hillside to the south began in the early 18th century. Most of the planting which makes it so famous to-day, however, has been done in the first half of the present century by Sir James and Lady Burnett of Leys who presented the castle and gardens to the National Trust for Scotland in 1952.

The design is simple, a large rectangle of land divided into a number of smaller rectangles, some of which are deeply terraced to cope with the natural fall of the land. The upper terraces are protected by massive yew hedges, well over 200 years old and trimmed in various shapes so that they add materially to the attractiveness of the garden.

The various subsidiary gardens are sharply contrasted in style and planting. The uppermost is entirely formal, rather in the Dutch style, with little clipped hedges of yew, a central pool and well-filled flower beds. It stands next to a large lawn open and unplanted except for surrounding specimen hollies and conifers. Another formal garden is planted mainly with blue flowers, a fourth is a rose garden and a fifth has close island beds of shrubs. Long, sheltered borders between yew hedges and a terrace wall are planted with exceptionally choice shrubs, many of which might seem too tender for the locality but thrive admirably.

There is a particularly attractive garden with a magnificent specimen of *Prunus serrula* in the centre, spreading its branches over an old stone trough and surrounded by well-filled beds of shrubs and hardy plants. There are twin borders planted entirely to a grey and white colour scheme and another border, which runs diagonally across the lowest rectangle to centre on an ancient dovecot, is planted with hardy perennials to give a peak display in June.

But it is for the quality and richness of the planting throughout rather than for details of design that the gardens of Crathes Castle are chiefly memorable, for here will be found a collection of trees, shrubs and herbaceous perennials truly remarkable in a situation so far to the north-east, and comparable with many of the best in southern and western counties. Because of this variety the garden retains its interest throughout the year.

Cardiocrinum giganteum, *a mammoth lily, flourishing in one of the gardens of Crathes Castle*

Inveresk Lodge

Inveresk, Midlothian. In Inveresk, half-a-mile south of Musselburgh on the A6124 which links with the A68 from Edinburgh to Lauder. The National Trust for Scotland. Open daily, except Saturdays, throughout the year.

The National Trust for Scotland is restoring the little village of Inveresk as an example of 17th-century village architecture. This includes Inveresk Lodge as the principal house in the village, and since its garden was almost completely derelict, a new garden has been made with many modern features such as island beds of shrubs, and borders of floribunda roses, but designed overall in the spirit of the period. It all lies around the rim of a curling valley, which, adjacent to the house, has been terraced and walled, but in its outlying parts follows the natural contours of the land. In addition to the modern roses there is an excellent border of old-fashioned roses, as well as paved walks bordered by lavender, pinks and other old-world plants.

Leith Hall

Kennethmont, Aberdeenshire. Six miles south of Huntly on the A979 to the A96 north of Inverurie. The National Trust for Scotland. Open daily from May to September.

The garden is at some little distance from the house, on rising ground with good views over the neighbouring countryside. Until quite recently much of it was orchard and vegetable garden, but an extensive rock garden around a pool was made many years ago and is an attractive example of its kind, gaily planted with perennials of all kinds, including some that are more frequently seen in herbaceous borders than in rock gardens. It is built up into high mounds and from the top several fine views, both of the countryside and of the garden, are to be obtained.

This rock garden is approached through a wrought-iron gate and a gravelled path between some of the most colourful summer herbaceous borders to be seen anywhere. The variety of plants is not great, but they are planted in large groups of a kind for colour effect, especially in late summer. Other parts of the garden are

now being developed with roses, shrubs, annuals and other plants so as to increase its attractiveness and lengthen its season of display, thus providing greater interest for the visitor throughout the whole of the spring and summer.

Above left. The border of old-fashioned roses and lavender against a stone terrace at Inveresk Lodge

Above right. A colourful border of summer-flowering hardy herbaceous plants at Leith Hall, Aberdeenshire

Edinburgh Botanic

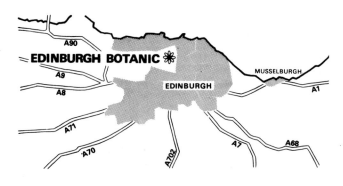

Edinburgh. On the north side of Edinburgh, off Ferry Road (A902) between Inverleith Row and Arboretum Road. Ministry of Public Building and Works. Open daily throughout the year except for Christmas Day.

Though this famous botanic garden, the second oldest in Great Britain, is packed into a rectangle of only slightly over 60 acres and is hemmed in by roads on every side, clever planning has made it appear much larger, and in some parts, such as the lovely woodland garden and the peat garden to which it leads, it is easy to imagine that one is far from any town.

The rock garden, built up to a considerable height on what is already one of the highest points in the garden, is one of the largest and best stocked in Europe and commands superb views of the famous Edinburgh skyline, with Arthur's Seat and the Pentland Hills in the background. Good views can also be obtained from the top of the knoll on which stands Inverleith House, and on the slopes of which are extensive plantations of rhododendrons.

There is an herbaceous border of exceptional length backed by a tall beech hedge behind which a most interesting series of demonstration plots has been laid out.

Other features of this garden are its large pond surrounded by moisture-loving plants, its rose garden and its many fine trees planted as specimens. But, in some ways, most remarkable of all is its latest acquisition, the new plant houses which have been built between the old palm houses and the new herbarium. These show an entirely novel approach to glasshouse structure since their roofs are suspended from outside rather after the manner of a suspension bridge. This results in a complete absence of interior supports or other obstructions and has permitted highly imaginative planning and planting of the available space. There is a large pool for the cultivation of *Victoria regia* and other tropical aquatics and, at a lower level, a viewing chamber from which visitors can peer into the water itself, see the manner in which the plants root and admire the tropical fish with which the pool is stocked. The largest section is devoted to plants from temperate regions requiring only frost protection, and others contain desert plants, tree ferns and a further selection of tropical water plants. Quite apart from its novelty, the building has considerable beauty and great architectural interest. The new herbarium is also a fine example of imaginative architecture.

Opposite. Meconopses, viburnums and maples at Branklyn

Below. Victoria regia *growing in one of the new plant houses at Edinburgh Botanic Garden*

Branklyn

Perth, Perthshire. On the south-east side of Perth just above the A85 to Dundee. The National Trust for Scotland. Open daily from March to the end of September.

The garden at Branklyn is small by National Trust standards, no more than 2 acres, and is now surrounded by other houses with the main road below, but it has been created with so much skill that it is one of the most perfect examples of its kind. It is a typically 20th-century garden, 'natural' in its intention, part woodland garden, part open scree, but because of its limited size everything has had to be kept under the strictest control.

This is a plantsman's garden in which many rare and beautiful species grow under conditions simulating as nearly as possible those they would enjoy in the wild. Much of the planting is very dense with narrow grass or gravel paths winding between informal beds following the contours of the hillside on which the garden lies. Yet 'wild' gardening gives a wrong impression of a garden in which every effect has been so carefully considered and no plant has been permitted to occupy an undue amount of space. Branklyn is, in consequence, a model for other owners of small gardens who would like to grow a considerable variety of plants without permitting their gardens to become overgrown jungles. It is a perfect example of the employment of ground cover to eliminate weeds and make the maximum use of available space, and because of the range of plants it contains it can be visited with pleasure at any time of the year. Nevertheless, it is in spring and early summer, when it is filled with the bloom of rhododendrons, azaleas, meconopses, primulas and lilies, that it is at its peak.

From its upper parts there are some fine views westwards over Perth and the valley of the River Tay.

Kincorth

Forres, Moray. Two miles north-west of Forres off the A96 to Nairn. Privately owned. Open Monday to Friday from June to August.

A pleasant modern garden of a type that might be seen around many a country parsonage or small manor house, but rendered memorable by the excellence and variety of the planting. A lawn, with a few trees and an enormous bush of *Rosa longicuspis*, laps around the house on two sides and leads to a simple rose garden between yew hedges which separate it from the vegetable garden. To one side of this, backed by a wall, is a very large and well-filled herbaceous border. On the far side of the drive the

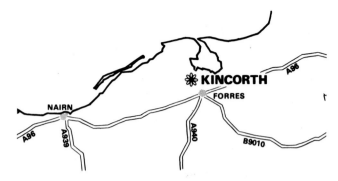

ground falls to a stream, and opportunity has been taken of this natural feature to create a little wild garden with drifts of astilbes and other moisture-loving plants near the streamside.

Falkland Palace

Falkland, Fife. In Falkland. The National Trust for Scotland. Open daily from April to October.

Gardening has been carried on at Falkland Palace for many hundreds of years, but the main outlines of the garden as it is to-day probably did not come into being until the 17th century. Within this framework, and partly with the aid of an old print showing the garden as it once was, an entirely new garden has been created in recent years under the direction of Mr Percy Cane. This combines the spirit of the old with good modern planting of trees, shrubs and herbaceous plants. The great lawn, beneath the palace walls, remains where it has been since the early 16th century, but is now encircled by island beds of shrubs and borders of herbaceous perennials, some of which are placed to carry the eye to the most dramatic or beautiful features of the palace itself. Beyond this lawn, separating it from the old covered tennis court, a charming formal garden has been created, paved and with a long, raised, rectangular water-lily pool running through it. As elsewhere at Falkland Palace, the planting of the walls with clematis and other climbers is a feature of note. On raised ground which was once part of the palace itself, a heather garden has been made, and from this vantage point there are some good views of the palace, the garden below and the surrounding country.

Above. The herbaceous border beside the vegetable garden at Kincorth

Right. Clever use of plants and paths to direct the eye to salient features at Falkland Palace, and opposite left, the formal water garden at Falkland Palace

Williamston

Insch, Aberdeenshire. Ten miles north-east of Inverurie on the A96 to Huntly. Privately owned. Open daily from June to mid-October.

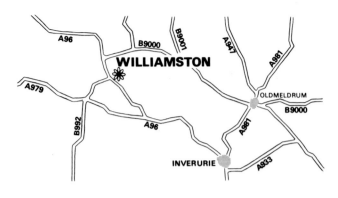

This comparatively small garden has been made to look much larger than it is by the clever use of long vistas both through and across it. Long hedges and square-cut columns of yew are used to channel these views which are also enclosed by twin herbaceous borders running through the kitchen garden. In contrast to these long and narrow views there is an open area of lawn treated as a little parterre with gay bedding plants and a statue. In addition to the more formal features of design there is a shrub garden with winding paths, again increasing the impression of extent, and a delightful little pool garden with a wishing-well, planted around with gunnera, candelabra primulas and other moisture-loving plants.

Two views at Williamston. Above, double flower borders through the centre of the vegetable garden, and below right, a statue set as a focal point to one of the long alleys of square-cut yew trees

Western Scotland

INVEREWE

A832

A835

A890

A9

INVERNESS

A82

A9

A96

ABERDEEN

A87

A86

A9

A92

A9

OBAN

A82

A827

A85

DUNDEE

A83

PERTH

KILORAN

CRARAE LODGE

A84

A9

STIRLING

BEN MORE

GLENARN

A82

A80

A9

EDINBURGH

A815

A8

A8

A1

GLASGOW

POLLOK HOUSE

ACHAMORE HOUSE

A77

BRODICK CASTLE

CULZEAN CASTLE

A74

A77

A1

GLENAPP CASTLE

DUMFRIES

STRANRAER

LARNE

LOCHINCH

A75

THREAVE

CARLISLE

LOGAN

miles

0 10 20 30

0 10 20 30 40 50 km

To those who are unaware of the peculiar effect of the Gulf Stream Drift on the climate of the British Isles, the gardens of Western Scotland come as a staggering surprise. For here, in a northern latitude which might seem to indicate bitter winter weather, many quite tender plants thrive. The explanation is that this coast is lapped by sea warmed from the Caribbean and, since it is a coast fretted with deep lochs, this natural heating system is carried far inland so that gardens of sub-tropical

luxuriance and variety can be made in many of the glens. Even as far north as Inverewe this extraordinary effect of the sea on plants is to be seen in a garden, which for sheer grandeur of setting is unsurpassed in the British Isles. It is seen, too, in the islands that abound off this coast, several of which, notably Gigha and Colonsay, boast gardens of supreme interest to plant lovers.

One of the best examples, in the British Isles, of an old landscape garden re-dressed with the finest modern plants is to be seen at Lochinch, Stranraer, while only a few miles away at Logan is another plant lover's paradise. There are many more.

Pool, palms and tree ferns at Logan

Achamore House

Isle of Gigha, Argyll. On the island of Gigha four miles west of Tayinloan (from which there is a ferry) on the A83 from Tarbert to Campbeltown. Privately owned. Open daily from April to October.

The island of Gigha is small and surrounded by sea warmed by the Gulf Stream Drift which has played so important a part in the development of west coast Scottish gardens. Achamore House stands in a fold of land facing east and is sheltered from Atlantic gales, both by the ridge behind it and by a thick belt of trees. Because of these natural and man-made amenities it has been possible to grow successfully a great many trees and shrubs usually regarded as decidedly tender in British gardens. Side by side with these are fully hardy plants chosen for their beauty or rarity, or both. The approach drive curves up to the house through wide lawns bordered by rhododendrons, azaleas and other exotic shrubs. Behind the house is a walled garden in which there are borders of roses, some old-fashioned tulips and other plants that like plenty of light and air, as well as greenhouses for plants needing even greater protection. But beyond this one quickly enters woodland thinned sufficiently to make room for an almost unimaginably rich underplanting of rhododendrons and other plants with, here and there, more open glades for primulas, and also a plentiful use of evergreen screens for greater shelter. These divide the woodland into numerous sections and there is a tendency to group plants of a kind within them, a system reminiscent of botanical planning. In fact, there is a strong element of the botanical about this garden and it is of interest to note that the plants it contains, though not the garden itself, have been presented by the owner to the National Trust for Scotland. Many are being propagated and used to re-stock other gardens under National Trust care.

Glenapp Castle

Ballantrae, Ayrshire. Two miles south of Ballantrae on the A77 to Stranraer. Privately owned. Open daily from April to October.

The house, in Scottish baronial style, occupies a wide terrace from which the land slopes away fairly steeply on two sides. It is surrounded by woodland and open parkland, much of the latter planted in the late 19th century with fine trees now grown to maturity. Immediately in front of the large house terrace are several smaller terraces, one with an old rose garden now considerably simplified in design from its original Victorian complexity, but none the worse for that.

At a lower level and to one side across the park, a lake, which forms a good landscape feature, has recently been almost completely surrounded with deciduous azaleas giving a splendid burst of colour in late spring and early summer as well as adding to the autumn colouring of the park. A path leads from this to the old walled kitchen garden which still retains a large conservatory and has been provided with double herbaceous borders as a new feature. Beyond this again the land rises steeply with massive outcrops of rock, and advantage has been taken of this naturally romantic setting to make a little stream and pool garden planted with candelabra primulas and other moisture-loving plants. Here, too, is an enkianthus of quite exceptional size.

The drive from the house curls downhill through the woodland which, below the azalea pool, is cut through diagonally by a burn in a little glen which offers scope for much further planting.

Right. A great drift of candelabra primulas backed by azaleas and rhododendrons by one of the pools in the woodland at Achamore House

Opposite top. A woodland glade planted with azaleas and libertia at Achamore House on the island of Gigha

Opposite bottom. Deciduous azaleas beside the lake at Glenapp Castle, which stands on a high terrace commanding a fine view of the garden and woodland

Pollok House

Glasgow. At Pollokshaws on the A736 from central Glasgow to Barrhead. Glasgow Corporation. Open daily throughout the year.

The house, built in the mid-18th century, is a fine example of the work of William Adam, and it stands in extensive parkland beside the River Cart, which is here spanned by an elegant stone bridge designed by William Adam's son, John. The garden is virtually in two parts, the original formal terracing to the south between the house and the river and, on rising ground to the east, an extensive 20th-century woodland garden.

There are two main terraces linked by stone steps, the upper flanked by stone pavilions of the same period as the house, the lawn with fine wrought-iron gates and semi-circular steps leading down to the riverside. The lower terrace, once an elaborate parterre, has been simplified to meet modern labour requirements, and is now filled mainly with grass plats, but the terrace walls are well planted.

Access to the woodland garden is by way of a formal

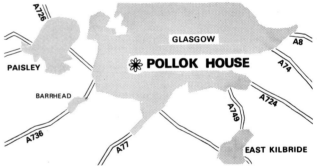

rose garden with beds enclosed in box. The woodland garden itself is rather more firmly designed than is usual, with a great beech tree on a mound in the centre, surrounded by a circular path from which other paths radiate through beds densely planted with rhododendrons and a great variety of other choice shrubs and trees. To the south, where the land slopes quite steeply towards the river, the treatment is much more open and there is a long walk bordered by daffodils. More daffodils in vast quantity are naturalised in a great tree avenue which extends northwards through the park from the entrance court of the house.

Logan

Ardwell, Wigtownshire. Ten miles south of Stranraer on the A716. Privately owned. Open on Sundays, Mondays and Wednesdays from April to September inclusive.

Logan is situated on the eastern edge of the Rhinns of Galloway, that narrow neck of land that projects from the south-western corner of Scotland into the Irish Sea like the head of a pick axe. It is a district noted for the extreme mildness of its climate, where potatoes are lifted almost as early as in the Channel Islands 400 miles to the south.

Gardening of a kind has been carried out at Logan for centuries, in the course of which many high walls of stone and brick have been constructed to give shelter from sea gales, but not until the present century was any attempt made to use this favourable site for the cultivation of a great collection of exotic plants, many of them from sub-tropical climates. It was left to the late Mr R. O. Hambro to try this experiment, which proved so successful that to-day the Logan gardens are amongst the most famous of their kind in the British Isles. Palms, tree ferns and cordylines have grown to such great size that it is hard to believe few of them are more than 50 years old. Embothriums from Chile blaze with scarlet flowers in May and there are great numbers of rhododendrons, some in bloom as early as January. Asiatic primulas have naturalised

themselves everywhere, even on the sides of a rough road that runs for half-a-mile through the woods to the beach, from which there are fine views across Luce Bay to the outlying hills of the Southern Uplands.

The gardens consist of a series of walled or hedged enclosures linked one with another, and an area of hillside planted as a rock and wild garden. In the old walled gardens free use has been made of sundials, wrought-iron gates, stone and terracotta ornaments and water, the latter in formal pools and basins, so that the overall effect is rather that of a Mediterranean garden. There is an impression of great age, partly due to the size of many of the plants, partly to the old walls and terraces and the fragmentary ruins of a mediaeval castle. It is hard to remember at Logan that one is really in Scotland and not bordering the Mediterranean, because of the effectiveness of the planting.

ℬenmore

Benmore, Dunoon, Argyll. Four miles north of Dunoon on the A815 road to Strachur. The Ministry of Public Building and Works. Open daily from April to September.

This is an extension of the Edinburgh Botanic Garden acquired specifically for the purpose of enlarging the collection of rhododendrons. The river linking Loch Eck with Holy Loch flows down one side of the garden. The site is nearly level with minor undulations for a short distance and then rises sharply up the foothills of Benmore. There is good cover of evergreen and deciduous trees and from the entrance gates a magnificent avenue of redwoods, said to be the finest in Scotland, leads towards the house, which does not form part of the botanic garden but is used as an adventure centre by the Glasgow Municipality.

An artificial lake and island have been formed on the lower land. To one side there is a large rectangular formal garden, mainly grassed, but surrounded by shrub borders, with long narrow borders of dwarf conifers running through it, and a golden boy on a dolphin in a circular basin as a central feature. This garden is backed by another, much smaller one, which is dominated by a large fountain and basin with female figures, all in white marble, and by a high wall against which blocks of tufa stone have been set and

planted with heathers, bergenias, etc., so that the whole wall is clothed from top to bottom. Beds in this little garden are filled with astilbes, skunk cabbage (lysichitum) and other moisture-loving plants.

All these features are ancillary to the main garden and are intended to extend its interest after the rhododendrons in the woodland and on the hillside have finished flowering. The layout here is simple and conventional, with the rhododendrons placed singly but grouped according to their series, i.e. their botanical relationship. Good use has been made of the natural features of the site, especially on the hillside where outcrops of rock provide natural settings for the low-growing species and hybrid rhododendrons.

Opposite. Terrace and stone pavilion at Pollok House

Below. Steps leading to the goldfish pond, Younger Botanic Garden, Benmore

Culzean Castle

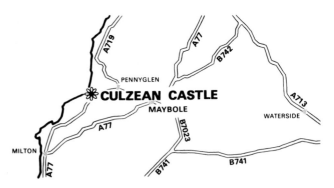

Maybole, Ayrshire. Three miles west of Maybole on the A719 from Ayr to Milton. The National Trust for Scotland. Open daily throughout the year.

Culzean Castle is not of mediaeval origin, but is an elaborate, castle-like mansion built by Robert Adam in the late 18th century. It stands on a cliff top overlooking the sea, a fittingly dramatic setting for this highly fanciful building, and its several gardens have something of the same romantic quality.

Behind the castle there is a little valley which has been levelled and terraced to make a formal garden. The deep retaining walls on the castle side are battlemented, but the far side remains a steep bank topped by trees and largely covered by heathers. In the centre is a handsome bronze fountain in a large scalloped basin which itself stands in a cross-shaped pool, for which reason this garden is known as the Fountain Court. Palms thrive in it, the terrace walls are well planted and at one end is a handsome orangery.

At some distance, reached by a walk through woodland past a camellia house, are two walled gardens, side by side, once presumably devoted to fruit and vegetables and now flower gardens, one being bisected lengthwise by twin herbaceous borders, the other mainly lawn with specimen trees and shrubs.

From this point the scene becomes rapidly more wild, the paths dividing, one to enter a woodland glen, known as the Happy Valley, the other leading to a pavilion beside a large lake, known as the Swan Lake. These outlying parts of the garden have been very neglected, but offer great scope for reclamation as woodland and waterside gardens.

The Fountain Court beneath the walls of Culzean

Inverewe

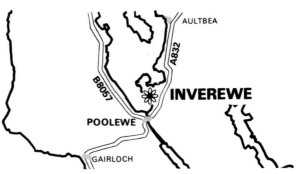

Poolewe, Wester Ross. Half-a-mile north of Poolewe on the A832 road to Aultbea. The National Trust for Scotland. Open every day.

This is one of the most northerly of the famous British gardens, but despite its latitude it is by no means a cold garden since it lies beside Loch Ewe, a sea loch warmed from the Atlantic by the Gulf Stream Drift. But though Inverewe does not suffer much from severe frost it is exposed to the full violence of Atlantic gales and the rocky peninsula on which it stands has little natural soil, what it does possess being of the most barren and acid nature. It was, therefore, an enormous achievement to create a garden there at all, and to establish a garden of the size and quality that now exists was little short of a miracle. Work was started in 1865 by Mr Osgood Mackenzie, who continued to plant and enlarge the garden until his death in 1922. After this his daughter cared for the garden until she handed it over to the National Trust for Scotland in 1952.

The rhododendron collection is one of the most extensive in the British Isles and a great many other exotic plants thrive, including dog's-tooth violets (erythronium), meconopses, gentians, candelabra and other primulas, celmisias and watsonias. The published list of species thriving in the garden is impressive and reads like the index of a botanical treatise.

The garden lies on two small hills and in the saddle between them, falling to the water's edge on both sides of its narrow peninsula. The views across Loch Ewe and to the mountains flanking Loch Maree are magnificent, and suitable viewpoints have been provided on the perimeter of the garden from which they can be enjoyed. Little use has been made of these views in the design of the garden itself, which, like others in exposed places, has had to be encircled with evergreen trees and shrubs to make possible the cultivation of any choice plants. In fact, apart from the viewpoints, this is a rather enclosed garden with few open spaces, but plenty of paths, some sufficiently wide and straight to provide fairly extensive vistas, leading through dense plantations of shrubs and herbaceous plants. Only around the house, which is tucked into the hill-side facing south-west, is there more open treatment, with curving lawns and stone terraces dropping steeply to the sea.

Glenarn

Rhu, Dumbartonshire. At Rhu off the A814 from Dumbarton to Garelochhead. Privately owned. Open daily from March to August.

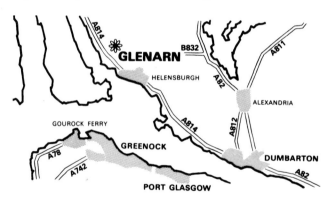

This is a plantsman's garden sited on a hillside behind Rhu facing west, with fine views across Gare Loch. A little glen, so narrow as to be almost a ravine, cuts down the hill beside the house which stands on a terrace, one of the few level places in the garden. This ravine has proved an ideal place in which to grow a great many rhododendrons and magnolias, including some of the most difficult kinds.

On the other side of the house the steep slope leads up through beds of meconopses, primulas and many rare alpine and herbaceous plants to a delightful rock garden, part natural, part man-made. Ascending still further one passes through a gate to the greenhouses, in and around which more rare plants are grown, finally reaching a little plateau which leads back to the top of the glen. Here are more primulas and rhododendrons, the latter dotted about in an open, park-like manner in contrast to the jungle-like profusion of the glen.

Among the many rarities that thrive in this remarkable garden are the Chatham Island forget-me-not (*Myosotidium nobile*) and the fragrant *Daphne petraea* of which Reginald Farrer said that it was 'only to be collected after long and sedulous search by very superior persons'. This is characteristic of a great many plants at Glenarn.

Above. Primulas and meconopses at Inverewe. The path provides a vista to the mountains beyond.

Below. Rhododendron Royal Flush at Glenarn, a garden noted for its rare plants

Lochinch

Castle Kennedy, Wigtownshire. Three miles east of Stranraer on the A75 to Newton Stewart. Privately owned. Open daily from April to September.

Castle Kennedy is a ruin standing on a ridge between two large lakes, the Black Loch to the north-east and the White Loch to the south-west. More than half a mile away, at the end of the lochs, is Lochinch, a mansion in Scottish baronial style built in 1867 to replace Castle Kennedy as a dwelling house. The great landscape and woodland gardens lie between the lochs and around Castle Kennedy which makes a highly romantic focal point for them.

One's first sight of the castle is approaching from the village of Castle Kennedy by the long drive which runs near the White Loch, across which the dark, ivy-covered ruin can be seen almost surrounded by trees, except for an open avenue of embrothriums which leads up to it.

But the main glories of the garden are on the other side where the land falls gently to a huge depression, then rises more steeply to a ridge from which it falls again equally sharply to the Black Loch. In this great natural punch-bowl a large circular pond has been made and filled with water-lilies. All around are dense plantations of rhododendrons and azaleas, through which wide grass avenues have been left. The longest

of these, lined with monkey-puzzle trees (araucaria), leads to Lochinch, the candle-snuffer towers of which can just be glimpsed in the distance.

The grass slopes on the ridge facing Castle Kennedy have been terraced in semi-circular sweeps of grass, as if for an open-air theatre, and a little to the north a great circular grass bastion, known as Mount Marlborough, provides the most exciting views of the pond on one side and the Black Loch on the other. Wherever one goes in this garden one is conscious of this care to make the best use of the lovely views. All along the ridge running south-east from Mount Marlborough openings have been left in the planting of trees and shrubs, with flat look-out spots from which the various aspects of the Black Loch can be admired.

Throughout the planting is of the highest quality, many of the fine rhododendrons and azaleas having been raised at Lochinch. Because the climate is mild, many rather tender trees and shrubs can be grown and so the garden is of as much interest to collectors as it is to those who simply admire fine landscape gardening of which this is a good example.

Crarae Lodge

Crarae, Argyll. Three miles south-west of Furnace on the A83 from Inveraray to Lochgilphead. Privately owned. Open daily from March to October.

This is the most spectacular of the Scottish woodland gardens, partly from the nature of the site, a deep glen from which the little River Crarae erupts to flow into Loch Fyne only a few hundred yards distant. This turbulent burn has cut itself so deep a channel through the rock that the sides of the glen are, in places, nearly vertical cliffs, and the visitor can cross and re-cross from one side to the other on little wooden bridges which provide aerial views of the exciting things happening below.

For this really is a very exciting garden, because of the way in which all manner of exotic trees and shrubs have established themselves as if in their natural habitat. The climate is mild and damp, there is not a great deal of sunshine as there is at Kiloran (see p. 153), and not all plants appreciate this, but those that do thrive amazingly well. Rhododendrons and azaleas grow everywhere, even sprouting out of the apparently bare stone of the ravine. Further up, where the river behaves more like a normal Scottish burn, bounding along over a broad bed of stones, it is lined by deciduous azaleas which give it an altogether un-Scottish look.

Large-leaved gunneras seed themselves about in the damper places; on the higher and drier bluffs there are fine plantations of rare conifers, eucalyptus, eucryphias, embothriums and many other fine trees and shrubs and everywhere there is a jungle-like luxuriance of growth. May to June is the peak flower period at Crarae Lodge, but because of the very wide range of plants grown, there is something of interest from spring to autumn.

From the high ground to the south of the glen and also from an azalea-covered bluff to the north of the house there are magnificent views of Loch Fyne and the mountains of Stralachlan on the far shore.

Opposite. The romantic ruins of Castle Kennedy seen from the azalea-covered slopes of Mount Marlborough across the circular pool at Lochinch. This pool is shown above and has been constructed in a natural bowl *occurring between two lakes, the White Loch and the Black Loch*

Below. Azaleas beside the burn at Crarae Lodge

Threave

Castle Douglas, Kirkcudbrightshire. One-and-a-half miles west of Castle Douglas off the A75 to Ringford. The National Trust for Scotland. Open daily throughout the year.

Threave House and its gardens are used as a training centre for young gardeners, and to this end the gardens have been greatly developed since they were presented to the National Trust for Scotland in 1948. The site is undulating and well wooded, in part open parkland with good specimen trees as well as small coppices, mainly of pine and spruce. In one of the latter an excellent woodland garden has been made, planted not only with rhododendrons and azaleas, but also with a wide selection of other shade-loving plants including primulas, meconopses, lilies and hostas. There are two extensive rock gardens, one provided with an unusually fine and well-planted scree, the other largely planted with heathers and brooms. The large walled kitchen garden and glasshouses which it contains are also open to the public.

This is still a young garden though it occupies an old and well-developed site. Already it is of great interest and beauty, qualities which may be expected to increase as the garden matures.

Brodick Castle

Brodick, Isle of Arran, Bute. One-and-a-half miles north of Brodick on the A841 to Corrie. Steamer to Brodick from Fairlie or Ardrossan. The National Trust for Scotland. Open daily except Sundays from Easter to September.

Brodick Castle is a red sandstone building standing on the lower slopes of Goatfell, the highest mountain of Arran, and looking out southwards across Brodick Bay. It is an imposing house, built at different periods from the 14th to the 19th centuries and it has two separate gardens, also made at different times. The older is a rectangular walled garden made in 1710, severely formal in design, but following the natural slope of the ground. It is an open, sunny garden, now largely planted with roses, but with some beds reserved for plants requiring warm and sheltered conditions including a notable collection of fuchsias.

The other garden lies on the steep slopes to the bay some 100 feet below and has been entirely made since 1923. It combines woodland, water and rock and,

because of its wide range of conditions, from dry to wet, sunny to shady, an exceptionally varied collection of trees, shrubs, herbaceous plants and alpines has been successfully established in it.

Just below the walled garden is a pleasant pool garden in a little dell ringed by rhododendrons, azaleas and pieris, with gunneras planted at the water's edge, primulas running wild in the moist ground, and intriguing glimpses of the sea through the trees. Below this again the land falls steeply and a large rock garden has been made, traversed by a winding stone staircase, and very richly planted, not so much with alpines as with more primulas, meconopses and other plants that enjoy cool moist conditions.

From here the land plunges the last 40 feet or so almost to sea level, with a flat area below in which many of the finest large-leaved rhododendrons have been planted. To right and left of all these central features there are woodland walks and great natural outcrops of rock, both with many plants of interest.

Kiloran

Isle of Colonsay, Argyll. One-and-a-half miles north of Scalasaig on A871. Ferry service from Tarbert West Loch (A83). Privately owned. Open daily throughout the year.

Kiloran is the most westerly of the famous Scottish woodland gardens and there is nothing but the Atlantic between it and the American coast. This, coupled with the fact that no part of the island reaches an elevation of 500 feet, accounts for its mild and exceptionally sunny climate, for the warm Gulf Stream Drift laps around it, and the absence of large hills means that little cloud formation occurs over the island. These features, combined with an acid soil and an abundance of soil moisture from a little stream that flows through it, have made the garden of Kiloran one of the best places in the British Isles in which to grow the more tender rhododendrons. Many other exotic trees, shrubs and herbaceous plants also thrive at Kiloran including palms, grevilleas, pieris, myrtles, embothriums, sophora and tricuspidaria. There is even a hedge of the beautiful and unusual *Desfontainea spinosa* used as a shelter belt to a little dell.

The garden occupies a shallow valley and follows the natural lie of the land with few formal features except a walled garden to one side, near the house, in which some of the most tender plants are grown. For the rest, it is entered by a farm lane which leads to a lake flanked by azaleas and other shrubs. Nearby, a little knoll with considerable outcrop of rock, has been converted into a natural rock garden with bold plantings of evergreen azaleas and Japanese maples. From the lake the stream rushes down a rocky cascade beside which is a bluff with an overhanging cliff covered with ferns. The stream enters the dell, which is full of rhododendrons, and then drops to the terraced lawns in front of the house. Facing these, on the far side of the valley, is woodland in which there are more rhododendrons, access being by narrow winding paths.

Opposite top. Rock garden and scree at Threave

Opposite bottom. The pond, Brodick Castle (left) and streamside garden, Kiloran

Northern Ireland

The Italian garden at Mount Stewart

*O*nly the narrow waters of the Northern Channel separate Ireland from Scotland and the geological features of the one are continued into the other. So it is not surprising to find that several of the most famous gardens of Northern Ireland are similar in character to those of Southern Scotland. For example at Rowallane, south of Belfast, many of the same plants will be encountered as those at Lochinch (see p. 150) and Logan (see p. 146). As at Logan, too, there is a walled garden in which many of the more tender varieties will be found, and a wild garden full of azaleas, rhododendrons and other fine shrubs.

But gardening came comparatively late to Northern Ireland and nothing will be found here of real antiquity as in so many of the Scottish gardens. Even at Mount Stewart, the most formal garden in Northern Ireland, some parts of which might seem to be very old, it will be found that a great deal of the work has been carried out in the last 50 years. This provides yet another remarkable example of the success of amateurs in garden making even on the largest scale, since the new gardens were entirely designed by the 7th Marchioness of Londonderry and executed by her and her garden staff.

Mount Stewart

Greyabbey, Co. Down. Five miles south-east of Newtownards on the A20 to Portaferry. The National Trust. Open on Wednesdays, Saturdays, Sundays and Bank Holiday Mondays from April to September.

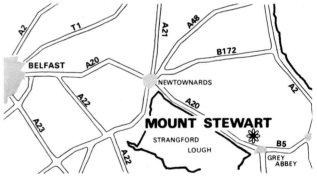

This is a very large garden covering nearly 80 acres; it has a complex and highly organised design and it contains an astonishing variety of plants, many grown to great size. It is difficult to realise that until 1919 there was virtually no garden at all at Mount Stewart, and that the whole conception is the work of one lady, making use solely of local labour, even for the numerous statues and ornaments that adorn it.

House and garden lie close beside Strangford Lough with the Irish Sea only about 4 miles away to the east, so that the situation is similar to that of a garden on an island. The climate is mild and moist and plants grow extremely fast.

The garden is in two parts: to the north of the house a series of formal compartments lie between the house and the Lough, and on the east side a park and woodland garden stretch from a lake not far from the house to a ridge some distance inland. This woodland garden is well conceived and admirably planted, but it follows, in the main, conventional ideas, except for a very unusual termination on the hilltop: a private burial ground laid out as a formal garden and overlooked by a high stone pavilion from which some of the finest views of the woodland garden can be obtained.

All the same it is in the originality of the series of enclosed gardens around the house that interest inevitably centres. The largest and most elaborate is in front of the west face of the house and is in the form of a parterre in the Italian style with a raised paved terrace around two sides. Flower beds almost fill the space, edged not only with box in the conventional manner, but also with many other small shrubs including hebes and heathers. These beds are filled with perennial plants and roses. Semi-circular stone steps lead down to a formal water garden backed by a green-tiled loggia. But what makes the whole thing so strangely unique is the variety of statuary with which the garden is decorated. There is a row of masks mounted on pillars with monkeys sitting on top. Dodos perch on the terrace, Noah's ark stands on a plinth, a dinosaur and some rabbits share the balustrade, and tall columns flanking the stone stairway are surmounted by curly-tailed lions.

To the north is a large sunken garden, at its best in spring, and beyond this a garden in the shape of a shamrock leaf enclosed by high yew hedges with strange topiary animals on top and more elaborate topiary specimens, including a harp, inside. This garden is paved, but out of the paving a hand-shaped bed has been left and planted with red heather – the Red Hand of Ulster.

There are many more of these unusual features, some of which might jar in a smaller garden or in one planted with less lavishness and skill. At Mount Stewart they are cheerfully absorbed in the sub-tropical luxuriance, and from contemplation of them the visitor can pass instantly to admiration of some rare and beautiful exotic, which abound throughout the garden.

Rowallane

Saintfield, Co. Down. One mile south of Saintfield on the A7 to Downpatrick. The National Trust. Open daily from April to June and on Wednesdays, Saturdays, Sundays and Bank Holiday Mondays from July to October.

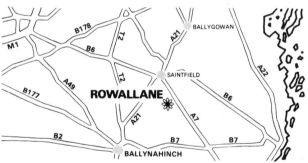

This is a specialised garden made, with the exception of a large walled garden near the house, with a minimum of plan and a maximum regard for the place in which each plant will thrive best. The climate is mild, the soil acid and stony, well suited to rhododendrons, azaleas and meconopses, of which there are notable collections. The walled garden, on level ground, is traversed by paths and is mainly filled with beds for plants rather in the style of a botanical garden, though there are also lawns and ornamental borders and some fine trees.

Beyond this the garden follows the natural, very irregular contours of the land, once evidently farmland, for the old dry-stone walls which divided one field from another still remain. The soil is thin and there are many natural outcrops of rock, some on a considerable scale. One of the largest of these has been made into a rock garden with a great variety of planting, from large shrubs, such as *Rhus cotinus* and Japanese maples, to quite small plants such as celmisias, lithospermums and creeping polygonums. Here, and

on other outcrops, meconopses are naturalised.

In less stony places there are great drifts of rhododendrons and azaleas, both evergreen and deciduous. Eucryphias, olearias and cornus all thrive and in some fields have been planted as isolated specimens to be viewed from all sides. There are good conifers, including one fine specimen of Brewer's spruce with its long weeping branchlets, and a great many more plants which could occupy the attention of a collector for weeks.

Opposite. The richly and permanently planted parterre in the Italian garden at Mount Stewart. Cordylines thrive in the mild climate provided by nearby Strangford Lough and the Irish Sea

Above. The rock garden at Rowallane, largely made on a natural outcrop of rock and planted with a mixture of alpines, herbaceous plant and shrubs

Acknowledgements

I am grateful to the following photographers and organisations who have supplied photographs of the gardens mentioned. Other illustrations included were photographed by myself.   *Arthur Hellyer*

AERO FILMS LTD.
Black and white: Tresco Abbey.

AMATEUR GARDENING
Colour: Charleston Manor, The Garden House, Haddon Hall.
Black and white: Barrington Court, Bedgebury Pinetum, Borde Hill, Chartwell, Clare College, Cliveden, Dawyck, Edinburgh Botanic Garden, Great Dixter, Highdown Gardens, Howick Hall, Wakehurst Place.

P. ASTLEY-RUSHTON.
Colour: Cothay Manor.

J. K. BURRAS
Black and white: Oxford Botanic Garden.

G. DOUGLAS BOLTON
Colour: Queen Mary's Garden.
Black and white: Parcevall Hall.

BRITISH TRAVEL ASSOCIATION
Black and white: Blenheim Palace, Bramham, Chatsworth, Culzean Castle, Falkland Palace, Levens, Logan, Melbourne Hall, Packwood House, Rockingham Castle.

COUNTRY LIFE
Black and white: Dartington Hall, Newby Hall, Rousham House, Scotney Castle, Trentham Gardens, Wilton House.

J. E. DOWNWARD
Colour: Westonbirt Arboretum.
Black and white: Anglesey Abbey, Bodnant, Claverton Manor, The Garden House, Great Dixter, Hidcote Manor, Hodnet Hall, Leonardslee, Luton Hoo, Scotney Castle, Tintinhull House, Valley Garden (Windsor), Wakehurst Place, Waterhouse Plantations.

FOX PHOTOS
Black and white: Sandringham.

GRAEME
Black and white: Syon House.

IRIS HARDWICK
Colour: Barrington Court, Compton Wynyates, Minterne.
Black and white: Athelhampton, Bicton Gardens, Buscot Park, Lanhydrock, Montacute House, Portmeirion, Powis Castle, Prior Park, Stourhead.

PETER HUNT
Black and white: Castle Howard, Montacute House.

A. J. HUXLEY
Colour: Queen Mary's Garden.

A. F. KERSTING
Colour: Compton Wynyates.
Black and white: Bateman's, Compton Wynyates (Title page), Tresco Abbey.

ELSA MEGSON
Colour: Hidcote Manor.

ROBERT PEARSON
Colour: Kew, Kiloran.

MESSRS PLANAIR
Black and white: Hopetoun House.

KENNETH SCOWEN
Colour: Inverewe.

HARRY SMITH
Colour: Alton Towers, Bressingham Hall, Cambridge Botanic Garden, Dartington Hall, East Lambrook Manor, Exbury, Kew Palace, Ness, Scotney Castle, Sissinghurst Castle, Sheffield Park, Valley Garden (Harrogate), Wisley.
Black and white: Benmore, Blickling Hall, Branklyn, Killerton, Valley Garden (Harrogate).

GRAHAM S. THOMAS
Colour: Duncombe Park, Saltram House, Shugborough, Trengwainton, Waddesdon Manor, Winkworth Arboretum, Wrest Park.
Black and white: Abbotsbury Sub-tropical Gardens, Blickling Hall, Lyme Park, Polesden Lacey, Sizergh Castle.

BERTRAM UNNE
Black and white: Harewood House, Rudding Park.

Index